6-9-80

The Decline
of U.S. Power

The Decline
of U.S. Power

(and what we can do about it)

The *Business Week* Team

BRUCE NUSSBAUM

EDWARD M. MERVOSH

JACK KRAMER

LENNY GLYNN

LEWIS BEMAN

WILLIAM WOLMAN

LEWIS H. YOUNG

HOUGHTON MIFFLIN COMPANY BOSTON 1980

Library of Congress Cataloging in Publication Data
Main entry under title:

The Decline of U.S. power (and what we can do
  about it)

  Includes index.
    1. United States—Foreign economic relations.
2. United States—Foreign relations.
I. Nussbaum, Bruce. II. Business week (New York)
HF1455.D4   337.73   80–10886
ISBN 0-395-29248-4

Printed in the United States of America

P 10 9 8 7 6 5 4 3 2 1

This book is partially based on material appearing in
the special issue of *Business Week* for March 12, 1979.

TO THE FORTUNATE FEW
WHO GET TO FLY CLOSE ENOUGH
TO ALPHA CENTAURI
TO FEEL ITS HEAT.

Contents

The Decline
of U.S. Power

Introduction

FOR THE FIRST TIME in its history, the United States is no longer
growing in power and influence among the nations of the
world. In fact, the United States is now in steep decline, and the
Pax Americana that shaped modern history since World War II
is fast disintegrating. By almost any standards, the country is
entering the decade of the 1980s as a wounded, demoralized
colossus, faltering in its stride on the international political
arena. At home, a recession threatens the nation, and double-
digit inflation and currency debasement sap its economic will.
Abroad, OPEC holds a knife to the throat of America's economy, so deeply dependent on foreign oil. Even America's clos-
est allies in Europe and Asia are now its fiercest competitors on
the international trade markets, and the United States finds
itself too weak to support its chosen friends in the Middle East
and elsewhere.

Without the strength and leadership of America, the world is
speeding headlong into the most dangerous period it has experienced since the 1930s. For the rest of the twentieth century,
no single country will be able to set and enforce the international rules that have been necessary, over the years, to assure
global peace and prosperity. The bipolar world of the 1950s and
1960s, divided between U.S. and Soviet spheres of influence, is
cracking up into a dozen pockets of competing rival national
groupings with dangerously shifting alliances. The never-
ending need to pay for higher-priced OPEC oil imports is spark-
ing an invisible, neomercantilist trade war that is bursting apart
the Western economic order. Germany, France, Japan, and

others now fight the United States to export on the world market while throwing up protectionist walls at home to aid local workers and industries. Quiet currency manipulation to gain competitive advantage is taking place just as governments are subsidizing national industries to cheapen export prices. Newly industrialized countries like South Korea, Taiwan, and Brazil, with low wage rates and the most modern factories, are challenging the older, industrialized countries in steel, textiles, shipbuilding, and even electronics for a larger share of world trade, which is, itself, growing very slowly. At the same time, every nation scrambles for the oil it needs for survival. The parallels between the explosive years between the two world wars grow more striking as each day passes, and U.S. leadership stumbles along, unable to change the course of the nation or the impending course of history.

So evident is the crisis in the decay of U.S. power that it is causing a major change in the parameters of national political debate. In the years since the United States turned inward following the shattering debacle of Vietnam, Washington politics have been debilitated by a series of self-defeating domestic disputes. Washington has been preoccupied with healing the political wounds of both Vietnam and Nixon's Watergate intrigue, and the attempt to re-establish the decency of government in the eyes of America's people has taken precedence over major economic and foreign problems. This focus has made it impossible for the United States to cut free from its precarious dependence on unstable foreign sources of energy, control the incredibly high double-digit inflation that erodes savings and fosters debt, rationalize the Byzantine tax structure, and adopt policies that promote investment and not just consumption.

This self-absorption is now ending. The 1980 presidential election and the entire decade that follows are likely to see the re-emergence of foreign policy as the primary political issue. Quite suddenly it is clear that the welfare of the country is dependent on what happens overseas, and the need for the country to act strongly within the international arena has become absolutely crucial. Because of the amateurish behavior of the Carter administration, the primary campaigns are bound to focus on the issue of strong leadership for America to guide the nation through the dangerous years ahead. The outlook is for a new guns-and-butter debate, deciding who will be the next President of the United States. If the decline in U.S. power is to be arrested, the nation's dependence on a dozen or so politically unstable OPEC countries must end, domestic economic policy must change in order to encourage investment and technological innovation, and the trend toward spending a smaller share of the federal budget on defense must be reversed. Foreign trade and exports have to be seen as vital national concerns and encouraged, and the dollar must be viewed at home, as it is abroad, as the symbol of America's economic strength and political will.

Just as important, the leadership of the country must change its concept of power itself. In the past, power has been narrowly defined in terms of military prowess. And the United States has been buffeted by a series of unnerving shocks that, although they have occurred mainly in the military sphere, have deep-seated economic and monetary roots as well. The erosion of power is in many ways the product of the failure of America's leaders to recognize the connections between political, economic, financial, and military events and to develop coherent policies that deal with them in an integrated fashion. It is impossible to talk about the decline of U.S. power without discussing the plummeting dollar and the defensive European and Japanese reactions, which are moving them away from the United States into protective enclaves like the European Monetary System. Nor is it possible to discuss inflation in this country without analyzing not only OPEC's continued raising of the cost of oil but the government's own easy-money behavior. U.S. prestige is falling abroad because of the rise of the Soviet Union to parity with this country in nuclear arms and also because of the decline of U.S. multinational corporations vis-à-vis German, French, Japanese, and British global companies.

The parallels between the decline of the United States and the dollar in the 1970s and the fall of Britain and sterling in the 1930s are astonishing. Just as Britain's industrial strength eroded in the late nineteenth and early twentieth centuries, to the point where it could no longer sustain sterling as the world's major reserve currency, so too is America's economic superiority waning as the dollar sinks overseas. Sterling was knocked off the gold standard in 1931; the dollar was cut loose from gold just forty years later. In the 1920s and 1930s, currencies floated against one another, and there was an economic war of competitive devaluations. Today, Germany, Japan, and the United States are also accusing one another of manipulating their floating currencies to seek unfair economic advantages. And as unemployment soared during the Great Depression when growth evaporated, forcing governments to set up mercantilist trade policies, so today the same pressures—induced this time by the energy crisis—threaten neomercantilist trade wars. "The trend toward a new mercantilism is simply the result of governments failing to respond adequately to slow growth," said Jan Tinbergen, the Dutch Nobel laureate in economics, and added, "There has been a tendency among export-oriented countries, particularly Germany and Japan, to make achieving a large balance-of-payments surplus a major policy objective." Jacques Maisonrouge, president of IBM Europe, went further: "Governments are becoming mercantilist. But they are caught between a rock and a hard place. On the one hand, governments are against protectionism. On the other, they face very serious employment problems that create national tensions."

The domestic and foreign failures of the past decade mean that the new guns-and-butter debate will be fierce. Already in Washington and in places around the country where primaries have taken place there are clear signs of the impending strug-

gle. Jimmy Carter is running against OPEC, the big oil companies, and once again Washington, D.C., in his re-election bid.
The administration's proposed legislation to prohibit the big oil
companies from buying up any other corporations with sales or
assets of $100 million or more is clearly an attempt to play to the
public's fury against the oil giants, which it blames for last summer's gas lines and this past winter's rise in home-heating-oil
prices.

Politics is certainly behind the attempt to blame the recession, unemployment, and inflation solely on the OPEC nations.
Although there is no question that OPEC's blind voraciousness
tipped the United States and the rest of the world into recession
twice in the 1970s, America's own internal economic and financial policies pushed prices to inflationary levels years before
OPEC struck. OPEC's actions this time around will probably
cost the United States an extra 2 percent in inflation by the end
of 1980, 2 percent in growth, and at least 800,000 jobs. But
before the straw broke the camel's back, the animal had been
maltreated for years before. Attempts by the Kennedy and
Johnson administrations to fight a war in Vietnam and to redis-
tribute income to underprivileged minorities at the same time
led to inflationary policies that still plague the nation.

The original guns-and-butter debate in the mid 1960s over
who should get a bigger slice of America's economic pie—the
military to fight in Vietnam or the minorities to gain from the
Great Society programs—was unfortunately resolved by the
government's trying to offer something to everyone at once.
The only solution was to run the printing presses. In the 1950s
and early 1960s, the rate of increase for consumer prices was
about 3 percent annually. By 1976 this had risen to 4.8 percent;
by 1977 it hit 6.8 percent; and by 1978 it reached 9 percent. In
1979 the consumer price increase rate had skyrocketed to 13
percent annually. If policies don't change in the 1980s, inflation
could easily reach 20 percent and above by the middle of the
decade.

But the need to find a scapegoat for domestic policy failures was made very clear by the memo Chief Domestic Adviser Stuart E. Eizenstat sent to President Carter right after his return from the Tokyo summit in July 1979. Referring to the gasoline crisis of the summer, he wrote, "I do not need to detail for you the political damage we are suffering from all of this." Eizenstat went on to gloat: "We have a better opportunity than ever to assert leadership over an apparently insolvable problem, to shift the cause for inflation and energy problems to OPEC, to gain credibility with the American people, to offer hope of an eventual solution, to regain our political losses." Eizenstat summed up by stating, "With strong steps we can mobilize the nation around a real crisis and with a clear enemy —OPEC."

The Republicans, of course, couldn't agree more with this analysis, but they are now focusing on the question of leadership, as the Carter administration cannot do. In fact, demands for a reassertion of U.S. influence around the world are cutting right across party and ideological lines. Conservatives like John Connally and Ronald Reagan, who are leading a Republican attack on the Carter administration over the conduct of foreign affairs, are being joined by such GOP moderates as Senator Howard Baker (R.-Tenn.) and George Bush. And although criticism from such hawkish Democrats as Senators Henry M. Jackson of Washington and Daniel Patrick Moynihan of New York are predictable, moderate party notables, such as Senators Adlai Stevenson of Illinois and John Glenn of Ohio, are also decrying the decline of the United States.

Overseas, the erosion of U.S. power has gone so far and has become so threatening that there is little actual debate about whether to try to stop it. "As I travel around the world, there is no question that U.S. prestige is being openly questioned and challenged," said Otto Schoeppler, chairman of Chase Manhattan Ltd. in London. "Iran has simply added fuel to the fire that was already there. There is also a parallel decline in standing and prestige of U.S. companies in international markets. One feels this not only in manufacturing and consumer goods but even in my own business. The American banks are no longer dominant to the extent we were." And S. A. Constance, managing director of Manufacturers Hanover Ltd. in London, went even further: the erosion of American power, he said, is "the most talked-about subject in the world."

The issues raised by the new guns-and-butter debate will define America's way of life for the rest of the twentieth century. The contest will be fought over both policies and tactics, and the outcome will be determined by alliances among powerful groups within the country, with the middle class holding the pivotal position. The most crucial points will be:

• Will the United States continue its retreat from the international arena into self-destructive isolationism, or will it re-emerge in the 1980s and recognize that the future welfare of the nation depends on foreign trade, a strong dollar, stable supplies of energy, and an effective military presence?

• Will the United States continue to allow its economy to stagnate and to strive for a solution to its social problems by allowing those with political clout to determine how the benefits, however sparse, of this economy are to be divided, or will it shift to a high-growth economy, which generates more wealth for a greater number of participants?

• Will the U.S. Government continue its antagonistic position toward U.S. multinational corporations, or will there be a new period of cooperation among government, business, and labor that can produce the economic policies needed to compete with Japan Inc. and Germany Inc. on the world markets?

• Will the trend of retreating into the self, away from science and rational problem-solving, be replaced by a return to a view of the world as it is and the challenge of change and adventure that goes with conquering the frontiers of space, the seas, and, perhaps most difficult, the cities?

The outcome of the new guns-and-butter debate will determine the hard policy choices that must be made in the near future, and the choices will not always be clear.

Will individuals who supported the bid for lower taxes and the anti–big government thrust of Proposition 13 in California vote, instead, for higher taxes and greater government interference in their lives, which must result if a new federally sponsored synthetic-fuel industry is to be built so that the United States can be independent of OPEC? Will they welcome back the draft to rebuild the army after Vietnam? Will minorities accept a cutback in government programs as resources are shifted into long-term private investment?

The U.S. middle class is already reeling under the combined weight of double-digit inflation and heavy taxation. With the recession, unemployment is threatening millions of families who made the rational decision in an inflationary environment to go deeply into debt. Just when they are paying more money for higher-priced heating oil, these families face the loss of income when one or both wage-earners lose their jobs. In the end, the huge pyramid of consumer debt must crumble, and the first thing to go may be the heavily mortgaged house. The middle class this year wants big tax cuts to create jobs and save its homes. It can argue that, though inflation may be a problem and the dollar may be going to hell, unemployment and dispossession are far worse.

Corporate America may, in part, be an ally of this middle class. For years, business has been complaining loudly about the enormous growth of government red tape, which ties them up and curbs their power to invest. In this economy, capital investment has taken a poor second place to the satisfying of bureaucratic rules and regulations. The prospect of a reinvigorated federal government waving the banner of synthetic fuels in the name of patriotism, for example, may not be welcomed by those businessmen who want to see Washington's power cut back, not expanded.

This issue of growing government interference in the market economy may soon come to a head as pressure builds in the administration both to institute federal controls on capital exports overseas in an effort to support the dollar, and to establish wage-and-price controls at home in order to bolster the economy. "The Carter people have repeatedly said they won't do it [set up controls]," said Alan Stoga, an international economist at the First National Bank of Chicago. "But at the same time they don't hesitate to intervene in the economy. They don't trust the market very much. They haven't decontrolled gas and now we have the big government involvement in the synfuels thing."

Pitted against this side in the new debate will be the powerful military establishment and nearly all of the outward-looking corporations that operate on a global basis. These multinationals can only benefit from a revitalized American presence overseas, and many will profit from a new U.S. trade policy that equates exports with national prosperity.

Greater government aid to the multinationals in the form of tax credits can make them more competitive overseas with their European and Japanese corporate rivals. And demands by the United States for reciprocity on foreign direct investment, particularly in Japan, would be applauded by American companies that have found nontariff barriers preventing them from moving into rich markets abroad while the U.S. economy remains open.

The military and the multinationals will have to count on the middle class changing its sentiment toward government if they are to win the guns-and-butter debate, and it just might be OPEC that pushes this crucial segment of America to their side. The long gas lines and the soaring price of heating oil may have so infuriated the middle class and threatened its cherished and hard-won way of life that the demands for a reassertion of American power overseas will override its mistrust of, and anger toward, Washington. In fact, this important switch in middle-class attitudes may determine who wins the presidential election of 1980.

It is, of course, very difficult to pinpoint just when the United States began to decline in power. The country emerged from World War II with all the trappings of an imperial power, and it has had to live with the problems of empire ever since. America helped rebuild Europe through the Marshall Plan, but its ability to see, as it did then, the close links between the political, economic, and military sources of power was later lost, never to be exercised in relation to any other part of the world. In the wake of the application of a policy integrating economic and political goals in Europe, the United States and the rest of the industrial world experienced a remarkable economic renaissance; it turned the Depression of the 1930s and the warfare of the 1940s into memories (though bad ones) and laid the foundations for sustained stability and growth for the great industrial democracies for the next twenty-five years.

Cracks began to appear in the mid 1950s. The United States differed strongly with Britain and France when they invaded Egypt after that country nationalized the Suez Canal. The Europeans, long experienced in running much of the world, chafed under U.S. pressure to get out. Strains on the dollar began to develop by 1960 as the United States started running heavy current account deficits to support its military burden overseas. The United States complained that Europe and Japan were not paying enough for American troops stationed abroad as part of our mutual-defense treaties. Cuba highlighted another recurring problem of maintaining the American empire: an inability to channel the revolutionary process of radical economic and social change in the Third World to the benefit of the United States. And the Bay of Pigs fiasco in 1961, followed by the nuclear confrontation with the Soviet Union over missiles in Cuba, clearly demonstrated the danger of being sucked into Third World politics, which have become, increasingly, the arena for international competition. Nowhere was this more evident than in Vietnam.

Having taken on too large a share of the cost of collective security for the West, the United States discovered in Vietnam another of the ancient problems of empire: the high cost of defending or even properly defining its perimeters, especially perimeters without any immediate economic benefits to the mother country. With the Gulf of Tonkin Resolution of 1965, the Senate, with the exception of two members, followed President Lyndon B. Johnson in committing an unsuspecting American public to a major land war in Asia. The costs of this war for a society that was beginning to devote more and more resources to meeting the ambitious social goals of high economic growth, low unemployment, and racial integration began to produce economic strains—inflation and a weakened dollar—that have haunted the United States for nearly fifteen years.

The very first guns-and-butter debate emerged in the mid 1960s, when Johnson was confronted with the choice of financing either the Vietnam War or the programs of the Great Society. Unfortunately, he opted to finance both of them at the same time. Moreover, Johnson realized that it was (as it still is) politically difficult to hike taxes in America to pay for anything; it was especially troublesome when the taxes were intended to help pay for an unpopular war in the jungles of Asia. So he did not raise taxes to pay for either. Instead, he got the government to borrow huge amounts of money, increased the federal budget deficit, raised inflation rates, and started the dollar down the long road to weakness.

Nineteen seventy-three marked not only the humiliating retreat of America from Vietnam but the fall of the dollar from the gold standard. And while all eyes were on Saigon, a little-known group of Mideast nations, banded together as the Organization of Petroleum Exporting Countries, stabbed America in the economic heart by raising the price of oil fourfold. From the fall of Vietnam and the lightning blow of OPEC in 1973 to the fall of the Shah of Iran and the sharp hike in oil prices again in 1978, the United States has been in a self-absorbed mood of domestic political healing, and its role in the world arena has been cut back sharply. Unhappily, if ever there was an era when America could turn its back on the world and live peacefully and prosperously, that time is not now, nor will it ever be in the rest of the twentieth century. While the United States was turning inward, the country was becoming ever more dependent on the energy, raw materials, and markets of the outside world. And while it was debating its future role in the world, that international arena turned extremely competitive and downright hostile, with nations threatening to cut the supply of energy to America.

The stirrings of the new guns-and-butter debate on U.S. foreign policy come just a little more than a decade after the Nixon Doctrine was proclaimed on Guam, in July 1969. In substance, that doctrine called for the United States to cut back on its worldwide defense commitments while shifting part of the military burdens onto other nations. It recognized that the powerful U.S. economy could no longer sustain a war overseas, a social revolution at home, and the defense of Europe and Japan, all at the same time. This clear break with the containment policy of the Cold War and the "we shall go anywhere" policies of the Kennedy-Johnson era marked the first attempt to reduce and redefine the limits of American power in the world. Despite the continued U.S. involvement in Vietnam through 1973, when the last troops were withdrawn, and through 1975, when Saigon finally fell, this theme of limiting U.S. global power to narrow national interests was repeated again and again by Washington officials, especially former Secretary of State Henry Kissinger. In 1970, Kissinger said, "In many countries it looks as if the United States is in retreat, but we are doing what we are doing because we believe that if America is to remain related to the world it must define a relationship that we can sustain over an indefinite period."

Whatever the conceptual merits of the Nixon Doctrine, the United States failed to define its national interests successfully, and doubt about the nation's global leadership has become pervasive. Foreign leaders are confused about just what the United States considers important, much less vital, to the security and prosperity of the West, and trust in the ability of the United States to act decisively is at rock bottom. As proof, they point to the impunity with which Iranian students, acting with the approval of the Ayatollah Khomeini, invaded the U.S. embassy in Tehran and took as hostage sixty Americans (as well as some nationals of other countries) in November 1979. That action, aimed at forcing Washington to return the fallen shah, nearly triggered an international financial crisis when the Iranians began to remove their $6 billion in deposits with American banks in order, possibly, to mount an attack against the dollar. That, in turn, prompted President Carter to freeze Iranian assets, a move that shook the international monetary system. The hostage episode was but the latest in a series of moves that highlighted the decline of U.S. power, including the ease with which OPEC raises oil prices. And they point to the traipsing about of Cuban mercenaries throughout Africa; a Mideast peace treaty that neglects the Palestinians and winds up alienating the oil-rich Saudis; an American ambassador murdered in Kabul following a communist coup in Afghanistan; personal rebukes to the U.S. President in smaller countries like Mexico; and, of course, the fall of the Shah of Iran, the hand-picked ally of America.

Wounded by Vietnam and demoralized by Watergate, the United States has failed to come to terms with its own role as the world's leading power. But Iran demonstrated how the Nixon Doctrine was being vitiated by its own ambiguities, particularly since it set off massive oil-price rises and threatened the industrial world's basic energy supply. As a result, political necessities are forcing America to define more sharply the national interest and to make the initial moves to defend it.

In the near-desperate drive to ensure the safeguarding of
Persian Gulf oil after the upheaval in Iran, the White House has
now publicly acknowledged that it may be necessary for U.S.
troops to go into action in the Middle East. A special task force
of 110,000 men, troops from the United States, is being formed
to have the capability of intervening in the Middle East. The
United States is sending $200 million in arms to North Yemen,
a pro–Saudi Arabian state on the Persian Gulf, following a flare-
up of its long-standing war with Marxist South Yemen, which is
heavily advised by East German and Soviet military personnel.
Defense Secretary Harold Brown went on a swing through
Saudi Arabia, Jordan, Israel, and Egypt to reassure those nations. They may have been more than reassured. Following the
60 percent run-up in OPEC oil prices for 1978, the United States
sent messages to certain Mideast countries, hinting that the
military take-over of the oil fields remains an option if in the
future OPEC acts in a way that threatens America and its allies.

Performance, of course, is the key to the reassertion of American power. When Brown returned from his Mideast trip he also
said, "Our friends there will wait to see our performance." But
performance is what is missing from nearly everything the
Carter administration and previous administrations have attempted. Nixon's Project Independence, designed to make the
United States free of foreign control over the country's energy,
failed miserably. Rockefeller's plan to set up a $100 billion En-
ergy Bank never got off the ground. The attempt by the Carter
administration to create an $88 billion synthetic-fuel industry is
being chopped up in Congress. Decontrol of gasoline production and sales has been ruled out, despite the fact that it is one
of the easiest and quickest remedies to America's energy
crunch. In 1972, the United States imported 28 percent of its oil,
and by the end of 1978, the amount had soared to 48 percent.
Although Carter has promised to put a cap on the amount of
imported oil moving into the United States, nothing will be

accomplished except the cutting back of economic growth unless new sources of energy are found.

On inflation, the Carter administration has made a stand for
a "moderate" $29 billion deficit in the current budget. Yet the
recession is certain to produce a budget deficit closer to $60
billion, and may go as high as $100 billion if the government
continues to cut taxes and pay out unemployment benefits. And
inflation remains dangerously high, although it is down from
last summer's peak of 13 percent. Once the economy begins to
pull out of the recession and to expand, inflation will start off
again from a new plateau of higher numbers, and rates close to
20 percent may be in the offing in the months ahead.

The foreign exchange markets have already discounted a
mild recession for the United States in valuing the dollar and
are looking beyond to the policy reactions of the Carter administration as the presidential election draws near. No one
overseas has any confidence that, as unemployment rises and
the election draws near, the Carter administration will hew to
tight fiscal and monetary policies. Instead, the other countries
expect to see an opening of the money floodgates. The economy
would ride high for a short time but would then drown in a
wave of inflation.

There are good reasons for this doubt about America from
abroad. The retreat of U.S. power around the world goes much
deeper than a simple crisis of leadership that could be resolved
with a new administration. For nearly a quarter of a century,
from the end of World War II to the late 1960s, the United States
was the creator and leader of a remarkable world economic
system that produced wealth on a scale never before seen. And
it is this entire global system that is now in crisis. Unlike earlier
world economic and political empires, which were closed units
based on tight territorial control and heavily regulated mercan-
tile trade, the United States–built system was an open economy.
Its guiding principle remains the free flow of capital and goods

among nations via the market mechanism, although the encroaching protectionism of neomercantilism is now threatening.

Beginning with the Bretton Woods Conference of 1944, the United States deliberately constructed out of the ruins of the war an international monetary order based on the dollar as the world's reserve currency and providing for the free convertibility of all national monies. With the value of the dollar fixed to gold, and with all other currencies pegged to the dollar, the stability necessary for financing trade and development was assured.

But more than that, the United States fought to bring down tariff barriers and controls on trade around the world, and encouraged the setting up of the Common Market to create one huge free market. Through the Marshall Plan, the United States launched the rebuilding of the European economies devastated by World War II, and helped Japan rebuild as well. With its nuclear umbrella and armed forces, the United States stood ready to guarantee this open economic system against threats from the Soviet Union on the outside and enemies on the inside that might close off markets and needed resources, such as oil. As both banker and cop, the United States was the guarantor of the postwar global economy.

And though the new wealth benefited most of the nations within the system, the United States received special advantages. With the dollar as the world's reserve currency, and all other currencies fixed to it, the United States soon found it was able to run continual international payments deficits and—unlike all other nations—did not have to tighten up on its domestic economic policies to solve the problem. Foreign countries were all too willing to accept and hold dollars for years, since they were pegged to gold. In effect, this permitted America to export its inflation. By the 1970s, it was helping to finance the growing government deficit and to keep interest rates down, because foreign governments took their excess dollars and invested them in U.S. Treasury bills, to a point where they now own one third of the U.S. Government's outstanding obligations. Indirectly, the role of the dollar permitted the United States partially to finance its Vietnam War and Great Society programs by going into debt and getting foreigners to pick up its IOUs.

The dollar soon became overvalued under the Bretton Woods system. Although this made foreign imports cheaper in the United States, it also permitted U.S. multinational corporations to move abroad and buy very cheaply into the burgeoning European markets. Today, overseas profits account for one third or more of the overall profits of most of the top 100 multinational corporations and banks of the country.

The postwar economy that America built also benefited from American control of vital energy resources. Of the seven mammoth oil companies that came to control the oil wealth of the Middle East, five were United States–based. Control of this oil meant incredibly cheap energy for Europe and most of the world for twenty years—years when Europe's war-ravaged economy was being rebuilt. Unfortunately, oil companies producing domestic crude in alliance with both Republican and Democratic administrations managed to limit sharply imports of cheap foreign crude into the United States during those decades while they pumped out higher-priced domestic oil. And today, when there is tremendous need for domestically controlled energy, that oil is simply not there. But even so, the real cost of electricity actually fell in the 1950s and 1960s, and the decline did much to keep the economy growing.

Of course, there were burdens for the United States to bear for supporting this open economic system. Heavy military expenditures came from U.S. taxes that Europeans and Japanese did not have to pay, and wars were fought mainly by the United States. Yet the benefits of one massive global market were immense, and U.S. corporations profited, along with the rest of the Western world.

But the policies set in motion during the Vietnam War years are now imperiling the way of life built up since World War II. The military retreat that began with the defeat of the United States in a faraway Asian land that held no natural resources or markets threatens to undermine the nation's ability to protect the vital oil supply and the energy base of the global economy. Vietnam may have been seen by many as a place to defend America's word and commitments; the Middle East is clearly essential to the very economic security of Europe, Japan, and the United States. The overthrow of the shah, put in power by the CIA in 1953, is sending tremors throughout the royal families of Saudi Arabia, the United Arab Emirates, and elsewhere around the Persian Gulf. The weakness shown in America's inability to protect its chosen ally emboldens members of OPEC to launch new oil-price hikes again and again. Threats by the Palestinian radicals, who were again forgotten in the recent Camp David peace treaty between Israel and Egypt, are forcing more moderate Mideast countries, like Saudi Arabia and Kuwait, to use oil as a political weapon against the West. Dependent on large Palestinian populations for the actual running of their government bureaucracies and economies, and afraid the Palestinians may turn against them at any moment, the moderate royal families are giving in to demands for higher and higher prices for oil to force the West and Israel to accept the Palestine Liberation Organization (PLO) and a legitimate Palestinian state.

Occasionally, there is a small indication of honesty on the subject, as when Saudi Oil Minister Sheikh Ahmed Zaki Yamani said, "I do not think you expect Saudi Arabia to increase oil production to a very high level while we have the Palestinians living in tents."

In fact, it is the nation's precarious dependence on oil that most severely threatens its way of life and limits its power. Twice in the 1970s, price increases by OPEC caused economic slowdowns, first in 1974 and again in 1979. Each time large hikes

in energy prices were added to an already inflationary international economic environment. And each time governments had
to tighten monetary policies to the point of curbing economic
growth and raising unemployment.

The first OPEC price hike produced a major international
financial crisis. OPEC oil revenues shot up from $28 billion in
1973 to $106 billion a year later, with OPEC surpluses jumping
$6.5 billion to $68 billion. The private banking system, largely
through the Euromarkets, was able to recycle the petrodollars
to Western nations and less developed countries (LDCs), which
ran up enormous balance-of-payments deficits to pay for the
higher-priced imported oil—though just barely. LDCs were especially hard hit and found themselves wallowing in huge debts
—debts to Western, particularly American, banks—which they
threatened to default on as the squeeze on their finances continued through 1975. Fortunately, the recovery in the United
States, Japan, and Europe between 1976 and 1978 saved these
countries and, indirectly, the banks and the international financial system, but everyone came out of the 1974 recession finan-
cially weaker. The 1980 recession will again put strains on the
LDCs.

The major impact of the first OPEC price action was to raise
the *price* of oil. The price hike acted as a massive sales tax that
redistributed income from the West to the Middle East. The
United States shipped out $8 billion in 1973 to pay for oil. In
1979, the sum came to $60 billion. The recent OPEC action,
however, is even more serious. Although prices went up 60
percent between December 1978 and July 1979, the OPEC
action the second time around threatens the very *supply* of oil
to the United States and its allies. As Rimmer de Vries, senior
vice-president and chief international economist of the Morgan
Guaranty Trust Company, said: "The new oil situation is much
more a matter of limited future oil supply. The prospective oil
supply may not be adequate to meet potential demand at current prices . . ." And that, of course, threatens to place real limits

on the long-run growth prospects of the world economy. This, in turn, could mean much lower growth and much higher unemployment in the 1980s.

In the past, the ever-higher price for oil mandated by OPEC could at least be expected to generate greater amounts of oil around the world. Production of North Sea oil and Alaskan oil would never have been considered economical had it not been for the higher oil prices. But now, higher prices for energy are no longer any guarantee of greater amounts of oil. The OPEC nations have discovered that they can manipulate the price of oil by keeping supplies tight; what they lose as revenue in terms of lower volume, they gain in higher prices for their product. Last summer, glimmers of a return to some balance between demand and supply in oil began to take some steam out of the surging price of oil. But once the world's oil supply began to erode the price, six of the more militant members of OPEC immediately began to cut back production. Algeria, Kuwait, and Nigeria cut back their production by 10 to 25 percent, and Iraq, Iran, and Libya hinted that they were about to follow. The cutbacks sent oil prices up to the $18-to-$23 range agreed on in June, and some oil went for even more.

Behind this new OPEC move to control both the supply and the price of oil in the world is the decision by the Saudis to cease being the oil producer of last resort for the United States and the West. After tripling their oil production between 1969 and 1978, the Saudis have declared they will not produce more than 12 million barrels per day—ever—despite new oil finds. And only the Saudis, with more than 200 billion barrels of reserves, could produce the oil the United States will need in the decades ahead. No other source, including synfuels, can hope to match that amount.

Ostensibly, the Saudis are putting a cap on their oil production to help both themselves and America. For the Saudis, the 12 million barrel limit "maximizes our recovery rate and gives the world more breathing space for the day when the world oil supply runs out," said Abdul Hadi Taher, governor of Petromin, the Saudi national oil company. The Saudis also believe their action will force the United States to conserve oil, and that too will be in everyone's self-interest. "We think this is the balance needed to prolong reserves, and it also gives sufficient incentive to develop other sources of oil," Taher added. But Sheikh Yamani went further: "You have got to do it [conserve]. Oil is running out, and the Iranian disruption in supplies should be a real warning to you."

The one long-shot solution to the Saudi decision to restrict future oil production and prevent the possibly horrendous effects of such a restriction on the U.S. and Western economies lies with politics, not economics. The Arabs, of course, have always maintained that the key is the Palestinians. "The question of a comprehensive peace treaty that recognizes Palestinian rights and returns the Muslim holy places in East Jerusalem is so important, so emotionally felt by us, that it is the core of the problem," said Saudi Finance Minister Mohammed Ali Abalkhail. "Solve that, and all other problems disappear. Obviously we would give you more oil."

But no matter what happens to the Palestinian issue, the message is clear: the United States has become extremely vulnerable to foreign political blackmail because of its dependence on overseas oil. The U.S. tilt away from Israel toward the PLO also threatens to undermine whatever small gains were made at the Camp David talks last year. Israel is years away from direct talks with the PLO but fears oil pressure from the Arabs will push the United States to force it into early negotiations. So worrisome is the U.S. tilt that in the summer of 1979 Senator Moynihan warned the Carter administration not to bend under OPEC pressure. "American foreign policy is not for sale—not one million barrels of oil a day, not one hundred million barrels, will buy the honor of this Republic," said the senator. Just weeks before, the Saudis increased their production of oil by a million barrels a day for nine months, and both government and private oil company officials agreed that it was designed to pressure the United States to get the peace talks moving, this time with the PLO included. As the *Petroleum Intelligence Weekly* put it, "Whether the [1 million barrel a day] increment might continue, and at what volume, depends on decisions the Saudi leadership hasn't yet made. These will depend to a large degree on political considerations as well as the status of the world crude supply . . ."

If America's dependence on OPEC oil has grown over the years, Europe's and Japan's have jumped even more. Their vulnerability to a cutoff in OPEC oil is driving them to make their own deals. So afraid are Europeans that they will see their energy base cut out from under them that they are making plans to enter into direct discussions with the Arab OPEC nations to secure their oil lines. A long-term deal offering European technology, markets, and even weapons in exchange for oil is being contemplated by the nine members of the Common Market, led by France and six OPEC members, including Kuwait and Saudi Arabia. Such a deal could, of course, undercut the United States and at the least limit the supply of oil available on the world market. And if the Arabs get the Europeans to recognize a Palestinian state as part of the deal, then U.S. peace efforts in the Middle East could become unstuck.

This is clearly one of the major goals of the Arabs. "It would be highly unlikely that the two groups would sit down and the Palestinian issue did not come up," said one European official involved in the talks. And United Arab Emirates Oil Minister Mana Saeed al-Otaiba, OPEC's president, publicly stated that the talks "should not be limited to energy problems alone but should include political and economic areas of common interest."

Both Arabs and Europeans believe that there is much to be gained from lessening their dependence on the United States and its oil companies, and that this dialogue may be the way to do it. The Europeans have long argued that the industrialized countries' economic problems, especially inflation and the gyrations of the foreign exchange markets, are largely the fault of the United States and its lack of an energy policy. The dollar's decline is blamed for both the cut in OPEC's real income and the inflation that is threatening another recession in Europe.

The Europeans also have a strong bargaining chip in attracting Arab oil through the new European Monetary System. The EMS, dominated by the strong German mark and backed in part by gold, may become an alternative investment vehicle for recycling the OPEC cash hoard. Instead of keeping their cash in dollars, the OPEC nations may put it into the new European money, the European Currency Unit, or ECU. "The Arabs have frequently talked of tying oil prices to a basket of currencies, and I imagine that they would want to discuss what role the EMS could play if they should decide to cut loose from the dollar," said one Common Market official.

"There is a general sense that the United States does not know where it is going," observed an official of the Arabian American Oil Company (Aramco). "The French are now able to convince the rest of the European Community that, for a variety of reasons, the United States will not be able to challenge this initiative."

The European shift from a cooperative to a competitive economic and political stance with the United States has been played out, of course, most obviously in the financial arena. The dollar's fall has been the single most important issue of contention between America and its allies, and it is both symbol and cause for the break in the United States–dominated world economic order.

Runaway inflation and frequent payments deficits over the years have finally led to a chronic crisis of confidence in the dollar. Central banks, corporations, and individuals who, in the 1950s and 1960s, were only too willing to hold dollars as a safe asset for twenty years are now fleeing the currency. The breakup of the Bretton Woods fixed-rate system in 1973, when the United States took the dollar off the gold standard, has produced an ad hoc, volatile, floating international monetary system. The apparent desire of the Carter administration in 1977 actually to have the dollar go down against other currencies, in a naïve attempt to help U.S. trade competitiveness, has led to a crisis of confidence in the dollar as a reserve currency. "Talking down the dollar" became a favorite public pastime for certain Treasury officials who didn't foresee the dollar crashing when foreigners took them at their word. Since 1970, the dollar has been weak and has depreciated nearly 50 percent against the German mark, the Swiss franc, and the Japanese yen. Billions in cash have flowed out of dollars into these currencies, as well as into gold and even into commodities, as hedges against ravaging currency debasement.

The decline of the dollar has become so chronic that it has changed the entire position of the United States within the world economy. For the first time, the United States has been forced publicly to change its domestic monetary policy because of the dollar's behavior overseas. The decline proved so rapid in 1978 that an impending crash of the world's financial system pushed the Federal Reserve Board, on November 1, 1978, into raising interest rates to defend the currency. This was perhaps one of the most important events in the recent history of the country. The international position of the dollar suddenly became a burden to domestic policy, rather than an advantage to it. And despite the recession, interest rates have been kept inordinately high by the Fed's chairman, Paul A. Volcker, for the same reason—dollar weakness abroad. In earlier times, interest rates would have been lowered much more sharply to combat recession and restimulate the economy. To many overseas who clearly remember how the erosion of sterling, the world's reserve currency for 100 years, produced a deadly stop-go economy in Britain for decades, the action of November 1978 and current policy are chilling.

The decline of the dollar goes far beyond the international

financial system itself. As always, it is tied to global political and military factors. American soldiers on station in Germany or Japan who can't afford proper clothing or food hardly arouse confidence in the people they are supposed to be defending— or fear in those enemies they are supposed to be watching. "The biggest reason we've lost our zip is the decline of the dollar," said Raymund A. Kathe, a senior vice-president of Citibank in Japan. "We wasted ourselves in Vietnam. Now we've got too many of our dollars abroad that sooner or later we'll have to redeem, and you can't maintain a military abroad when people won't accept your currency."

Gold, of course, has been the primary beneficiary of the wasteful spending habits of the United States. During the first three years of the Carter administration, its price more than doubled, to an amazing $875 an ounce by January 1980. Individual Americans who were prohibited from owning gold for decades before 1974 are now flocking to the yellow metal to protect themselves from inflation and the debasement of their own currency. The United States has become the largest gold-trading center of the world, with more gold traded on the two commodity exchanges in Chicago and New York than even in London or Zurich. People are buying hundreds of millions of dollars worth of Krugerrand one-ounce coins, South African, Canadian, and American gold-mine shares, as well as gold futures contracts every year.

Despite all efforts by the U.S. Government to demonetize gold and convert the precious metal from its historic role as a store of value into a simple hunk of yellow metal, gold has grown in importance for the international monetary system. While the United States sells gold from its own Treasury to increase the supply and lower the price against the dollar, investors continue to buy the metal, pushing prices even higher. Foreign central banks are purchasing more and more gold, and the oil-producing nations of the Persian Gulf have started to barter secretly some of their precious metal. The

What undermines U.S. international influence

Accelerating inflation

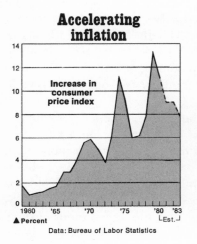

Increase in consumer price index

Percent

Data: Bureau of Labor Statistics

1960 '65 '70 '75 '80 '83
Est.

An eroding dollar

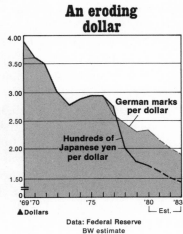

German marks per dollar

Hundreds of Japanese yen per dollar

Dollars

Data: Federal Reserve
BW estimate

'69 '70 '75 '80 '83
Est.

A shrinking defense commitment

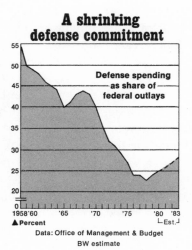

Defense spending as share of federal outlays

Percent

Data: Office of Management & Budget
BW estimate

1958 '60 '65 '70 '75 '80 '83
Est.

Saudis are believed to be swapping oil for gold with the South Africans, and the Russians too may have to deal with them. Recently, the Saudis were rumored to be selling twenty barrels of oil for one ounce of gold to the South Africans, and there is talk that many Mideast countries want to peg the price of oil to gold, especially if the dollar keeps declining.

In Europe, where gold has always been seen as a store of value in times of inflation, gold has been remonetized to the point where it is now included as 20 percent of the reserves of the European Monetary System, and many observers believe that the ECU may develop as a gold-backed European currency in the future if the dollar continues to erode and the world moves closer to a multireserve-currency system.

All these enormous strains are beginning to split the global economy into competing regional blocs as Europe and Japan strive to defend themselves from the effects of what they perceive as increasing American weakness. Currency blocs based on the mark and yen are developing while the erosion of the dollar proceeds, and protectionism is rising not only abroad but within the United States as well. International trade is suffering; it was cut from an annual rate of growth of 9 to 10 percent in the 1960s to only 5 percent in 1978 and a paltry 4 percent the year before. The EMS, built around the German mark, is quite clearly a defensive reaction, taken to construct a zone of monetary stability against the volatile dollar. Japan is turning to China and Southeast Asia for markets that it is losing because of the "voluntary" export limits imposed on it, via the new mercantilism, by America and Europe, which are more and more protectionist. Nation after nation, from Saudi Arabia to Thailand, is unpegging its currency from the soft dollar and is latching on to the yen, the mark, or some trade-weighted basket of currencies to protect itself from the falling U.S. currency.

So far, the United States has made a few gestures toward reasserting its power overseas, but all of them have been strictly in the military sphere. It is trying to put into place a 3 percent real increase in military spending for the first time in nearly a decade; there is the special task force set up to intervene, if necessary, in the Middle East; there is talk of a new fleet to patrol the Indian Ocean and guard the strategic Strait of Hormuz, through which passes much of the oil going to the United States, Europe, and Japan. But there is very little attention being given to the financial and economic sources of American power overseas.

In fact, the Carter administration, like most administrations before it, has shown little understanding of the political importance of a strong dollar or the strategic meaning of a strong American corporate presence overseas. No one in the administration seems to understand that the economic base of U.S. military strength is as important a projection of general U.S. power around the world as the number of missiles the country has aimed at the Soviet Union. "Inflation has hurt us all over the world more than anything, and we're afraid to face up to it," said Henry Harnischfeger, chairman of the Milwaukee-based Harnischfeger Corporation, a manufacturer of construction and mining equipment. "When the dollar is devalued, this is a reflection of the lack of confidence in the dollar and evidence that we really don't know how to run our own house. The world is looking to the United States for leadership, and we aren't giving it."

Harnischfeger knows what he is talking about. His company lost $20 million in 1978 on the cancelation of a contract with Iran after the shah was overthrown. The corporation also lost millions more on its German operations when the dollar plummeted against the German mark. So grievous were the losses that Harnischfeger almost had to sell his company to the huge German construction firm Mannesmann when the German company offered a high price for the stock. For the Germans, with their strong currency, the price of the American company was relatively cheap. In the 1970s, the overvalued mark permitted the Germans to buy into the American economy just as deeply as the overvalued dollar allowed U.S. corporations to buy up European assets right after the war. The trend will continue in the 1980s.

Unfortunately for the United States, the ability to exert global influence through economic and financial power is clearly understood in Bonn and Tokyo, where governments huddling under the American nuclear umbrella make their presence felt in nonmilitary ways around the world. Moreover, both the Germans and Japanese value the close contacts between government and big business because they see investment abroad and exports as extensions of national influence. While the U.S. federal government prosecutes American corporate executives for "bribing" foreigners to get overseas contracts for American companies, German, Japanese, French, British, and other governments aid their own companies through cheap credit and even political wheeling and dealing in the competitive fight for foreign business. Recognition of governments, cheap trade financing through national banks, votes in the UN, support for foreign interests, are all part of the bargaining European and Japanese governments use in gaining business for their own multinational corporations. America, undoubtedly because of a tendency to project its post-Watergate morality overseas, has neglected the financial and business realities required for the exercise of international influence.

To reverse this, the U.S. Government may have to call off its "war" against those of its own multinational corporations that are losing business to European and Japanese rivals. "We can't operate out here if we have laws that were passed by do-gooders that put us at a competitive disadvantage," said Citibank's Kathe. Kathe complained that the Japanese, British, Germans, and French are making strong headway in investment and trade in Asia—long a U.S. bailiwick—because they are not shackled by antibribery and antiboycott laws or by environmentalist pressures.

The United States has no way of escaping the costs of the

current crisis of power. It calls for hard choices in every area where vital interests are at stake: the Middle East, the dollar, energy policy, multinational corporations, and the military. The government and the country will have to prescribe policies that may not be easy for many groups in America to accept. Policies, based on the experience of the Depression, that pump up demand in the economy may now have to be changed to emphasize increasing supply. The dollar can no longer be allowed to float wherever the foreign exchange markets take it, and a return to managing currencies is inevitable. Resources may have to be switched from social spending to research and development. Tax policies may have to be altered to encourage investment rather than consumption. And foreign policy may have to be changed specifically to highlight vital U.S. interests and outline what the country must do to protect them. Above all, a national consensus of where the people are heading is needed, and the forces that were unleashed to land a man on the moon must now be harnessed to get the nation to fight for its future.

The Pivotal Middle East

A Struggle for More Than Oil

The Stakes

In the Middle East, America is faced with a double-edged sword. One edge cuts at U.S. strategic interests, as ideologies and power blocs vie for supremacy and the Soviet Union in particular seeks advantage. The other cuts to the quick of America's vital economic interests as the oil on which the West depends falls ever further into jeopardy. These dangers have been illuminated with stark clarity by the explosion in Iran, but they are hardly confined to that nation.

Following the Iranian revolution in 1979 there were reports of an abortive coup led by Saudi air force officers in league, or at least in touch, with Iranian Revolutionary Affairs Minister Ibrahim Yazdi. Given the secrecy and tight controls on news in the kingdom, it is impossible to confirm or discredit such reports. But reliable sources inside and outside Saudi Arabia confirm that there is radical Muslim-nationalist sentiment directed against the royal family—despite the family's espousal of equal Muslim orthodoxy and nationalism. Perhaps more important, the Camp David peace treaty was seen by many Muslim nationalists as an unbearable compromise with the West. Since the pact was signed, there has been a distinct, if far from complete, estrangement between Saudi Arabia and the United States, and there have been ground-breaking discussions between Saudi Arabia and the Soviet Union.

The Soviet Union is going to become a net importer of oil by the mid 1980s, according to the CIA, and arrangements for

importing Saudi crude may be under way. The entry of the
Soviet Union into the world oil market, of course, can only take
away that much of the precious energy source from the United
States, Europe, and Japan, and push prices even higher.

A vast, global shift in political alignments could occur if control of the Persian Gulf's oil were to fall into hostile hands. Japan
especially depends on the oil that comes from the Middle East.
If that oil were to be appropriated by a power inimical to the
United States, Japan might have to abandon the relationship it
now has with the United States. (At the Tokyo economic summit in 1979 the Japanese cautiously advanced the Arab cause.
Prime Minister Masayoshi Ohira graciously proposed that the
heads of the world's seven leading industrial nations draft a
joint resolution calling for recognition and respect for the rights
of Palestinians.) And several west European countries would be
almost equally vulnerable to blackmail or, at least, to foreign
suasion. "There would be a dramatic shift in the regional balance of power," said former Energy Secretary James R. Schles-
inger, who is more a geopolitician than an energy expert.
"Given their dependency on that part of the world, Japan and
western Europe would have to change their orientation."

At the very least, the pull from antagonistic blocs would create enormous drag on the Western economic system. Indeed,
such pull is already being exerted on a number of Mideast
nations, most particularly Turkey. Heavily in debt to the West,
but unable to sell enough of its goods in Western markets, either
because they are inferior or because of trade restrictions, the
Turks are being lured eastward by the Council for Mutual Economic Assistance (COMECON) bloc. The Soviet Union and its
allies, accustomed to low quality and eager to win Turkish neu-
trality, are making deliberate efforts to cultivate Turkish trade.

Should the oil that industrial economies need fall into hostile
hands, the nature of the pull on these nations would be the
same: strain, perhaps unbearable strain, on the commercial ties
that bind together the West and Japan.

Right now it is sharply evident that U.S. power and influence in the Middle East has eroded, perhaps critically, and that the area is plagued by instability.

The Battleground: Camp David and the Mideast Triangle

On the map this crucial region in crisis is a neatly delineated triangle defined by Turkey at the northwest corner, Ethiopia and the Horn of Africa at the southern corner, and Afghanistan at the northeastern corner. At its epicenter is the world's largest supply of oil, a reservoir that forms an arc through Saudi Arabia, Kuwait, Iraq, and Iran. Three portentous trends clearly isolate the countries contained in this triangle from their Third World and European neighbors: the decline of U.S. influence, the rise of Soviet influence (both are present elsewhere but not nearly to the same degree), and a groundswell of puritanical Muslim fervor. As if this were not enough, the triangle is also marked by crucial geographic coincidence: at each of its three corners are strategically vital straits. In the northeast are the Bosporus and the Dardenelles, which bottle up Russia and have long made the Russians thirst for a warm-water port. In the south is the Strait of Babel Mandeb, which can squeeze shut the Red Sea and thereby the Suez Canal, cutting off most Asia-bound traffic of such countries as Israel, Ethiopia, the Sudan, and Saudi Arabia, including the latter's great entrepôt of Jidda and its vast budding port, Jubail. Indeed, the contest for this critical waterway has already begun. The 1967 Six Day War began after President Gamal Abdel Nasser of Egypt declared the Red Sea closed to Israel. And today the Israeli navy maintains an active interest in the Babel Mandeb passage, far from its shores. Before the fall of Ethiopia's emperor, Haile Selassie, it secretly occupied a nominally Ethiopian island near the strait, and its missile boats still patrol the region.

Not far from the triangle's northeast corner is the Strait of Hormuz, which can be used to close off the Persian Gulf and consequently shut down Saudi Arabia's remaining port of Dhahran, stopping all traffic out of the gulf states and some 40 percent of the free world's oil supply.

In a sense the hard strategic significance of this triangular slice of real estate is a reminder of the days when wars were fought for spoils and high ground. During the Cold War, and more recently in Angola and Ethiopia, abstract notions sparked conflicts. In particular, maneuvering between the United States and the Soviet Union has been largely ideological. In the Middle East, on the other hand, oil supplies and strategic straits are crucial in their own right, quite beyond any Marxist versus free world political considerations.

Unfortunately, however, this does not mean that a simple nineteenth-century compromise, defining practical spheres of influence, would settle the region. There is also an ideological battleground: the dispute between Israel and the Arab world. This dispute has been dangerously catalyzed by the Camp David accords. It can be argued that the accords were well worth the risk, that Arab-Israeli negotiations had been going nowhere for decades and something bold had to be done to break the logjam. In the meantime, though, the move has put enormous strains on the relationship between Saudi Arabia and the United States.

This is especially ironic, because Saudi insistence on progress in negotiations clearly spurred on the United States in its efforts to engineer a settlement. Unfortunately, America vastly misjudged what the Saudis could accept and their ability to lend political support to any settlement. Given enormous religious and Palestinian pressure, there was no way they could associate themselves with an agreement that virtually ignored East Jerusalem and the Palestinians. Contrary to popular American opinion, the Saudis' great wealth is not matched by political clout in the region defined by Istanbul, Kabul, and Addis Ababa at its three corners.

The Exposed Saudis and Their Gulf Allies

At the center of this almost perfect triangle sits a booming modern metropolis cast in the image of Dallas, Texas. Riyadh, the capital of Saudi Arabia, has knocked down most of the mud walls that characterized old King Ibn-Saud's seat of power, replacing them with sprawling vistas of concrete and steel, but the footings of the capital can hardly be called solid.

This is not to say the Saud dynasty is without its strengths. Unlike the regime of the shah, who was politically isolated and almost wholly dependent on the army for support, the Saudi monarchy is a more open system that provides ready access for those with grievances and enables the rulers to detect signs of trouble. Every Saudi has the right to take his problems personally to King Khalid, and ministerial offices are crowded with people bringing complaints. "You work for them," said Abdul-Aziz al-Zalel, chief of the Saudi Arabian Basic Industries Corporation (SABIC), the agency that promotes development. "If you are not providing them with electricity or water, you need to be reminded every day." Unlike the tens of thousands of Iranian students who stayed abroad to protest against the shah, their Saudi counterparts usually return home to well-paid jobs after finishing their studies.

Even so, the Saudis are nervous. They have taken precautions to try to keep discontent from boiling up, particularly among businessmen and the middle class, as it did in Iran. One likely move is a crackdown on corruption, which will probably be accomplished by the removal of a few officials as a warning. "They all have outside business interests," a knowledgeable observer said. "We would see it as a conflict of interest, although they don't. There must be some resentment growing." As a first step, a recent law limits agents' fees, through which most payoffs are made, to 5 percent, and military contracts are now negotiated directly with the government rather than through agents.

To make sure that small business men, who financed the revolution in Iran, do not feel that they are being left off the gravy train in Saudi Arabia, the Saudis have set up a special council with small business men among its members, to review major projects. "When you try to industrialize very quickly you often don't have the patience for working with the smaller business man; you get a Parsons or a Morrison-Knudsen [the Ralph M. Parsons Company and the Morrison-Knudsen Company] to attack the whole project," observed Ronald F. Reilly, a vice-president and specialist on Mideast affairs in Houston's Texas Commerce Bank. "Now they may be more inclined to break the projects down to smaller bits so local construction companies can get a share."

In the longer run, though, there is still a big question hanging over the Saudi ruling clan. "Is the monarchy an institution that can outlast the twentieth century?" asked Robert J. Pranger, director of foreign and defense policy studies at Washington's American Enterprise Institute. He added, "Capitalism tends in the direction of republicanism or constitutional monarchy." Some top Saudis also acknowledge that the tide of history is running against the present monarchical system, although they believe it can adjust to change. One such adjustment, in response to the upheaval in Iran, could be the appointment of a consultative council made up of prominent young Saudis. Such a council was proposed by Crown Prince Fahd in 1975 and then dropped until recently, when the idea cropped up again in Saudi newspapers. There may also be a move to create town councils, made up in part by elected members. This idea was suggested by a British consultant in a recent report to the

Municipalities and Rural Affairs Ministry. The United States is quietly encouraging such steps.

In neighboring Kuwait, Crown Prince Saad al-Abdullah al-Sabah, who is also the prime minister, has been having talks with prominent Kuwaitis about reopening the once vociferous National Assembly. It was shut down in 1976, when deputies became too critical of the government's social policies, the power of wealthy merchant families, and the alleged corruption by cabinet members. Now the government is worried about the upheaval in Iran, partly because Kuwaitis failed to foresee the shah's downfall. Reconvening the assembly, and thus providing a forum for public debate, would give the rulers advance warning if similar troubles start to brew in Kuwait. Such a move is also hinted at by the freer discussion of issues in the controlled newspapers.

There are good reasons for the royal family's nervousness. Only 47 percent of the inhabitants of the country are Kuwaitis. Palestinian expatriates, a highly politicized group, may be stirred to new activity by Iran's pledge of strong support for the PLO. They make up a quarter of the population and hold high positions in business and government. In fact, they almost control the bureaucracy and the managerial group, according to a British banker who spends a lot of time in Kuwait. And an estimated 20 to 30 percent of Kuwaiti nationals, including some large merchant families, are Shiite Muslims of Iranian descent who still speak Farsi and are generally not regarded as "real" Kuwaitis by other citizens. "In their hearts they belong to Khomeini, because they are not satisfied as citizens here," one Kuwaiti observed. "Now they will express their feelings more openly."

More serious may be a growing feeling among both Saudis and Kuwaitis that material prosperity is not enough. A Kuwaiti educator put it this way: "The main question is whether the royal families around the gulf are ready to share some of their power. Either they give in, or in the long run they will lose everything."

In Saudi Arabia fear of losing everything is what keeps the royal family from becoming openly fractious. Family members are supremely aware of the importance of presenting a united front and protecting the monarchy. If the monarchy goes, they all lose. Therefore, the royal princes guard their privacy and try to keep disagreements under their turbans. Yet, despite their caution, rumors of a serious conflict persist, a conflict that reportedly divides the family into two competing factions.

Recently, a series of events made the talk of a rift more credible. Crown Prince Fahd (who has been running the country since 1975, when his brother, King Khalid, authorized him to do so) unexpectedly flew to Spain for "health reasons." Khalid then resumed a more active role, taking charge of state affairs. This caused great anxiety in royal circles, for it was thought the moves meant that Fahd was on his way out and that Prince Abdullah, the powerful commander of the national guard, was on his way up. The issue dividing the two was whether Saudi Arabia should continue to support the United States–sponsored peace negotiations between Egypt and Israel. Within the family, the drive for Arab nationalism and a cooling of relations with the United States is often championed by Prince Abdullah and his supporters, Foreign Minister Prince Saud al-Faisal, National Security Chief Prince Mutaab and the governor of Riyadh, Prince Salman.

Frequently countering Prince Abdullah in these intrafamily disputes are the pro-West members of the royal family, who advocate formal long-term security arrangements with the United States. This group is led by Crown Prince Fahd and includes Defense and Aviation Minister Prince Sultan ibn-Abdel-Aziz, Interior Minister Prince Nayef, and Harvard-educated Oil Minister Sheikh Ahmed Zaki Yamani. (The sheikh is not a member of the royal family, but is trusted by the inner circle of the royal family and is allowed to take part in these disputes.)

Abdullah's ardently pro-Arab faction, which is disillusioned with the United States, has been gaining influence, and Saudi support for Arab hardliners at the Baghdad conference opposed to the Egyptian-Israeli peace treaty is the best evidence of this. And though Abdullah is the hardliners' leading advocate, Khalid is the man responsible. Once thought impossibly infirm, Khalid has shown strength in his resumption of his kingly role, receiving King Hussein of Jordan and former President Ahmed Hassan al-Bakr of Iraq. His message to them was clear: they were to support punitive action against Egypt.

Most observers agree that none of the family feuding is intended to overthrow the monarchy. Indeed, the discreet containment of the feud shows clearly that all sides are eager to preserve at least a modicum of cohesion.

Yet all of the tensions have not been resolved, and informed observers of the Middle East forecast that before all this is over a shakeup will take place. In its most extreme form the shakeup could see Prince Fahd, disappointed and disillusioned by the turn in Saudi foreign affairs, take over at the Ministry of Foreign Affairs. Foreign Minister Saud al-Faisal would then be put in charge of Oil and Minerals, replacing Sheikh Yamani, who could become minister of planning. And Hisham Nazir, now minister of planning, would likely become ambassador to the United States. Some say this would mean a step up for Yamani. Others believe it would mean a step down for him. Still others say Yamani is already out as a key player. The best guess is that the ball is still in play. But no matter what, the pro-Arab who is cool to the United States, Prince Sultan at the Defense Ministry, is considered a very influential player, on his way up.

Right now Saudi capacity to produce crude oil stands at about 10 million barrels a day. Sheikh Yamani has insisted that Saudi Arabia has no firm plans to make the big investments in wells,

pipelines, and other facilities that would be required to expand
oil output beyond a sustainable daily capacity of 12 million barrels sometime in the eighties. Such meager development plans
may be as alarming for Western oil consumers, in the long run,
as the present slow-down of Iranian oil production.

Iran's oil fields will now flow at a rate of 3 million to 4 million
barrels a day, most observers believe—well below the previous
daily peak of 6 million barrels. The Khomeini regime may be
reluctant to bring back the hundreds of foreign technicians who
would be required to push production to full capacity, and some
of the ayatollah's advisers have been arguing that Iran should
conserve its oil and spend less.

But Saudi Arabia is the only country in the Middle East with
the potential for multimillion barrel increases in output. As
recently as 1977, the Saudis proposed raising their capacity to
16 million barrels per day, a target later cut back to 14 million.
Now they say they do not intend to expand significantly unless
the United States is able to reassure King Khalid, Crown Prince
Fahd, and others in the royal inner circle that the United States
will be able to protect Saudi Arabia from aggression, either by
other Mideast countries or by Soviet-inspired regimes on the
periphery of the region. "We have to get our heads together
and start looking at the bear," said Deputy Planning Minister
Faisal Basheer.

The Saudis have scant manpower to defend themselves, regardless of how much military equipment the United States
sells them, so they also want the United States to help achieve
a broad peace settlement between Egypt and Israel that will
ease the tensions between Arab militants and moderates. Beyond that, they want the United States to curb its appetite for
oil. "Saudi Arabia will continue its responsible oil policy, but
consumers on their part can be less wasteful," said Abdul-Aziz
al-Turki, the Saudi deputy oil minister.

It will be difficult, though, for Washington to satisfy these
concerns fully. The Saudis are afraid that if they expand produc-

ing capacity, the United States and other consuming nations, instead of conserving energy, will immediately put pressure on them to produce the extra oil. But if the Saudis do not maintain a margin of spare capacity, they will lose their power to influence price decisions in the Organization of Petroleum Exporting Countries. That influence depends on their ability to threaten a sufficiently sharp increase in Saudi oil output to drive the world price down.

This dilemma may account for the discrepancy in the Saudi estimates of their sustainable producing capacity. Before the last OPEC meeting, Oil Minister Yamani claimed that Saudi Arabia could produce a sustained 12 million barrels per day. U.S. officials believe that the lower figure, around 10 million barrels, is correct, although the Saudis can produce up to 12 million for a limited period. If so, the Saudis are producing close to their maximum sustainable level right now. They recently raised to 9.5 million barrels the allowable daily production from the concession of Aramco, the operating company in which four U.S. oil majors still own an interest. On top of that, Saudi Arabia produces around 300,000 barrels a day from the neutral zone bordering Kuwait, and a roughly equal amount of liquefied natural gas.

The king and his brothers, led by Crown Prince Fahd, will eventually decide whether and when to install equipment to add to capacity, but a long-running debate in the Council of Ministers reflects the basic issues. Planning Minister Hisham Nazir, Finance Minister Mohammed Ali Abalkhail, and Industry Minister Ghazi al-Gosaibi argue that the kingdom should produce only enough oil to meet its current revenue needs and keep the rest in the ground to appreciate in value. On the other hand, Crown Prince Fahd, Princeton-educated Saud al-Faisal, and Yamani favor using oil as a political tool as well as an economic resource.

Politics, so far, has won out, but the Saudis feel that their already limited room for political maneuvering is dwindling in the current climate of Arab nationalism. "The Saudi royal family cannot be seen to run against the tide," asserted an international investment banker with extensive business ties in the Middle East. "Even if the Saudis agree to make up future oil shortfalls, they will then have to do it at substantially higher prices."

The outlook, therefore, is for only limited increases in oil output from the Middle East even if Iran goes back on stream, with resulting upward pressure on oil prices as world demand rises. Iraq, the only other country in the area that can boost output measurably, is expected to reach 4 or 5 million barrels per day, at most, by the mid 1980s, compared with current production of 3 million barrels.

The expanded revenues that higher prices are already pouring into Mideast countries, other than Iran, are one reason U.S. companies are generally optimistic about the prospects for continued business in Saudi Arabia and the gulf states, despite Khomeini's revolution. U.S. companies have steadily expanded their exports to the area even though oil production in recent years has leveled off. What that signifies, in part, is that the oil producers' expanding economies are able to absorb more goods and services, paid for with oil revenues that formerly were banked as surplus. One measure of this increasing absorptive capacity is the combined gross national product of Mideast countries, including Egypt and excluding Israel, which soared from $79 billion in 1973 to $206 billion in 1977, and probably continued to climb in 1978.

Starting in 1977, Saudi Arabia and the gulf emirates had slowed their breakneck spending pace somewhat to curb inflation and ease the social strains of rapid development. But what that means for Abu Dhabi, for example, is that budgeted spending is going up merely 30 percent in the current fiscal year instead of 80 percent, as in previous years.

Saudi Arabia's still-rising outlays actually created a current account deficit in the first three months of fiscal 1979, which started in June 1978, because oil production fell below the 8 million barrels per day that had been projected for that period. As a result, Saudi oil revenues dipped below the level needed to pay for imports under its $43 billion annual budget. That means, for one thing, that Saudi Arabia has lost some of its former ability to cut oil output sharply, if such a move becomes necessary to prop up oil prices in a sluggish market. Planning Minister Nazir formerly advocated lowering oil production to 5 million barrels per day or less to match revenues with import needs. At present oil prices, Saudi Arabia must now produce at least 7 million barrels per day to pay for imports; otherwise it will have to dip into its hoard of petrodollar reserves. Iraq, too, is becoming an important market. The Iraqis are plowing all of their oil revenues into development and buying increasing amounts of goods and services from U.S. suppliers.

But the troubles in Iran are prompting U.S. businessmen to look more closely at ways to hedge, when drawing up contracts, against losses due to tie-ups in deliveries and payments in other Mideast countries, and some are buying costly political risk insurance.

Iran's shift to orthodox religion is also seen in the Middle East as a lesson in trying to modernize too far too fast. The social upheavals unleashed by the shah's attempt to industrialize the country, and turn it into a major power by the turn of the next century, unleashed powerful forces that ultimately overthrew him. The traditional merchants of the bazaar were threatened by the new middle class. The banking system fostered by the government cut into their moneylending operations, and the large stores put up around the cities took away much of their trade. Allied with the Muslim hierarchy, which saw its lands taken away a decade ago, the bazaar merchants launched a counterrevolution against the shah and installed the mullahs. Along the way, those segments of the middle class which became politicized but were refused entry into the system by the shah joined the bandwagon from the left. As a result of the upheaval, Arabs throughout the Middle East are nervously cutting back their own modernization programs to prevent the waves of reaction in Iran from washing over their own borders.

U.S. companies are, however, still bullish on Saudi Arabia, the biggest U.S. market in the area. San Francisco's Bechtel Group, for one, is in Saudi Arabia on a long-term basis under a contract to manage development, over twenty years, of the $20 billion Jubail industrial complex. "The Middle East," according to Caspar W. Weinberger, former secretary of health, education, and welfare and now a Bechtel vice-president, "is still a busy, vital part of our business."

Many of the dangers that now abound in the region appear to march up to Saudi Arabia's doorstep and stop short. Soviet power is growing immensely, but it is unlikely that the generally prudent Soviets would court World War III by simply marching on the oil fields. Both Saudi Arabia and the gulf states have large, potentially flammable populations of expatriates, but they are rigidly controlled, and the indigenous populations of all these countries are the beneficiaries of generous share-the-wealth programs. Nonetheless, there is a two-pronged threat of grave potential danger to the United States. The first is that disaffected Saudi princes critical of forced draft development and caught up in the Islamic revival will find a model in the independent radicalism of Syria and Iraq. Such a move away from the United States will be all the more likely if the Soviet Union remains the dominant military power in the region. The second danger is that the current Saudi regime will see little reason to resist such pressure because in their eyes America has reneged on a tacit agreement, struck in 1974, that called on the United States to maintain a stabilizing presence in the region in exchange for a freeze on oil prices and the responsible management of the Saudis' huge hoard of dollars. Similarly in their eyes, they have yet to renege on their end of the bargain—and the West has yet to learn what that might mean.

The Decline of U.S. Influence

The United States is limited in the direct action it can take to shape the internal politics of countries in the vulnerable Mideast triangle. Not even the most hawkish critics of the administration suggest U.S. military intervention could have saved the shah, although many believe the United States could have—and should have—done more by covert operations, which are now virtually outlawed by the Carter administration and Congress. Some believe such operations should have been undertaken in support of the shah. Others believe they should have been undertaken to provide more alert intelligence of popular discontent and to spot a popular anticommunist leader early on.

In either case, a key reason little early action was taken was that the effect of declining U.S. influence in this sensitive Mideast triangle has tended to sneak up on Americans, both the administration and the public. For one thing, the region is not one most Americans think of as a natural arena of U.S. power. For another, ever since the United States overreached itself in its efforts to prop up its South Vietnamese clients, "policing" distant regions has been understandably unattractive.

Nonetheless, for years U.S. power and influence in the Middle East was real. And now the decline is real. The conservative nations of the region, on which the West depends for much of its oil, are feeling so isolated, and even betrayed, that it is impossible to predict the course of the price of oil and the uses to which Saudi Arabia might put its enormous cache of dollars.

Friendly Mideast governments are worried about the U.S. failure to resist what they see as a web of encirclement that the Soviet Union is weaving around them by setting up naval bases in the area and the massive support given to such hostile regimes as the Soviet-oriented People's Republic of South Yemen. The strain in relations between the United States and

Saudi Arabia, over this and other issues, became evident with Riyadh's cancelation of a visit in early 1979 to Washington by Crown Prince Fahd. It intensified when Fahd, while on an extended visit to Spain, made a secret side trip to Morocco to meet with Soviet emissaries. Shortly afterward, the Saudis granted the Soviets overflight permission for the first time. The move was especially troubling because most Soviet flights over Saudi Arabia are destined for South Yemen, which the Saudis have long feared as a base for subversion. Given the lack of U.S. support, the Saudis were clearly opting for appeasement as a means of coping with the Soviets. Indeed, the agreement was reached just a few short weeks after a truce was hastily patched together, cooling off a border war between South Yemen and the Saudis' clients in North Yemen.

Saudi diplomatic efforts have from time to time calmed tensions between South Yemen's fire-eating radicals and the more traditional regimes of North Yemen and Oman, and Aden has been obviously pleased by the Saudis' granting overflight permission to the Soviets. But there is little confidence that such appeasement will work in the long run, especially considering that the Saudis, despite their wealth and arms, are dealing from a position of weakness and fear: by some estimates there are almost as many Yemeni Arabs in the kingdom as Saudis, though no one can say for sure, because the situation is just too sensitive to permit a census to be taken. Along with other foreign laborers (including Shiite Muslim oil workers who owe allegiance to the ayatollahs of Iran) these Yemenis represent a potential fifth column of enormous danger.

United States–Saudi relations took perhaps their worst turn when the Arab states, including Saudi Arabia and its gulf allies, made it clear they were actually going to exercise at least some anti-Egyptian sanctions, which they had drawn up at the conference in Baghdad. One of the initial motivations of the Carter administration in pressuring the Israelis to make peace at Camp David had been Saudi insistence that the United States bring its influence to bear on the Israelis. Nonetheless, the actual shape of the treaty that emerged was so distasteful to the Saudis (in particular, they were upset about the failure of the accords to provide sufficiently for Palestinian interests and for the return of Arab East Jerusalem) that they would have preferred no agreement at all, and they set about to undermine it. This, in turn, upset the Americans and the Egyptians, who had become fundamentally committed to the peace process. On May Day, Egyptian President Sadat gave a landmark speech, lashing out at his Arab "enemies" and calling the Saudis "dwarfs."

Since that watershed address things have improved somewhat, but too much had already happened to permit any quick halt to the erosion of U.S. influence in the region. On the Middle East's northern flank, Turkey, with its vital role as anchor of the North Atlantic Treaty Organization, had been seriously undermined when, under prodding from the pro-Greek lobby, Congress cut off military aid to Turkey to pressure the Turks in their dispute with Greece over Cyprus. A wave of anti-Americanism in Turkey, and Ankara's shutdown of U.S. bases, led Congress to renew the aid in 1978, but Turkey's reliability as a NATO ally may never be fully restored.

Turks are fond of saying, "Nothing good ever comes from the north," a reference both to the weather and the Soviet Union, of which they are wary. But unlike czarist imperialists of old, the Soviets are acutely aware of Turkish sensitivities. Instead of challenging Ankara militarily, they are offering economic inducements. Over the past several years Turkey's efforts to fit into the Western economic system have resulted in a crushing debt burden, due in part to the Turks' inability to turn out goods that can compete in Western markets.

Recognizing the implications of the trend, Western nations have made extraordinary efforts to bail out the Turks with ever-larger loans. But the Soviets offer something else: a market for those Turkish goods the West won't buy. If the burden of Turkish debt ever becomes too great for the West to finance, or for the Turks to pay, the result could be a Turkish economic re-orientation to the East of more fundamental strategic significance than any military protocol.

In fact, on the Saudis' home turf at the Middle East's southern approaches, the Soviets are continuing to encroach on the fringes of the Arabian peninsula, while entrenching themselves in the Horn of Africa and steadily building naval strength in the Indian Ocean.

The Rise of Soviet Influence

The Soviets got their toehold in the Mideast triangle in 1967, when Marxists seized power in South Yemen, which includes the former British colony of Aden. They eventually allowed the Soviet Union to build a big naval base on Socotra Island, at the southern end of the Red Sea, giving the Soviets a commanding presence near the vital Strait of Babel Mandeb. Shortly afterward, the South Yemenis, armed and advised by the Russians and Cubans, lent their weight to a leftist guerrilla uprising in Oman, which could serve as a base for blocking the flow of oil out of the Persian Gulf at the Strait of Hormuz. The shah, armed and encouraged by the United States to police the gulf, sent troops to put down the Oman insurgents. Now that the shah has gone, there are fears that fighting may break out again. And despite periodic truces, South Yemen continues to threaten Saudi Arabia by attempting to subvert North Yemen (also called the Yemen Arab Republic).

At the same time, across the Red Sea, the Soviets and their Cuban clients are consolidating a massive presence in Ethiopia, where they are supplying arms, advisers, and thousands of Cuban troops to strengthen the United States–trained but Soviet-supported colonels who overthrew United States–supported Emperor Haile Selassie in 1974. Commanding the northern approaches to the strait, Ethiopia for years received more U.S. aid and guns than any other nation in Africa, and in turn used these resources to permit Selassie's Amhara tribe to control and suppress mercilessly the Tigre-speaking, Soviet-armed tribes in the south. Despite clear signs that it was propping an increasingly unpopular regime, the United States continued to support Selassie to the end, just as it did the shah. It paid for its lack of acuity when a radical military group called the Dergue overthrew Selassie and, miffed at U.S. refusal to continue arms supplies, turned to Moscow. In a shameless display of disloyalty, the Soviets abandoned the Eritrean and Somali movements, which had been struggling against what was virtually foreign domination, and jumped at the chance to replace the United States in Addis Ababa. It was a bold move, involving the risk of losing all credibility in the Horn. During the early months of the Soviet switch, both the Somali and Eritrean guerrillas won major victories. But it has paid off, largely because the United States remains committed to the policy that bound it to Selassie. Though there is no emperor left to support, the State Department feels it would be "inconsistent" even to express sympathy (and thereby issue a warning to the ambitious Soviets in Addis Ababa), let alone provide any marginal diplomatic aid for the "separatist" movements the United States once helped to combat. In the official U.S. view this would be contrary to the principles of the Organization of African Unity. In order to bolster themselves, the many shaky regimes that make up the OAU have enshrined old colonial boundaries as virtual holy writ, even though, often as not, they derive from straight lines drawn on nineteenth-century maps and frequently slice through tribal homelands, dividing some ethnic groups and casting others under alien rule.

Both Saudi Arabia and President Anwar el-Sadat are worried about the threat of Ethiopian-based subversion in the Sudan. Their concern is all the more justified by recent instability in Africa's largest state. There has been, reportedly, an unpublicized coup attempt against mildly pro-Western President Jaafer

Mohammed al-Nimeiry in recent months, and sources say the Soviets see the Sudan as Egypt's soft underbelly. Until last April the Sudan wholeheartedly supported Egypt's signing of a peace treaty with Israel. While maintaining that the treaty was not the whole answer to the Mideast question, Nimeiry nevertheless saw it as a start toward peace in the Middle East. However, he began toning down his all-out support for Egypt when the pressure from the hardline Arab states became too great. In late March, Iraq, which was under long-term contract to supply the Sudan with most of its oil, stopped doing so. Iraq says it cut off supplies because the Sudan was late in making payments. The Sudanese claim they had paid for the oil up front. In either case, Camp David undoubtedly played a role. The result was a hushed capital with traffic drawn to a near halt, snarled airline flight schedules, and virtually no fuel reaching the southern half of the country. Commerce was stalled for months as the Sudanese waited for new fuel supplies to arrive; Khartoum was forced to scurry for supplies. Finally, they got the Egyptians to send them an emergency supply and the Saudis to sign a long-term contract.

Being without oil shook the Sudanese. They started making conciliatory gestures to the hardliners while not entirely abandoning Egypt. Nimeiry sent a high-level Sudanese delegation to Libya in May to talk about rapprochement; for months the Libyans had been financing and even arming Sudanese dissidents. After the meeting, the Libyans claimed that the Sudanese had condemned the Egyptian-Israeli peace treaty and called for the restoration of Palestinian rights.

But the Sudanese president's problems are not only external. Nimeiry still has to contend with the opposition forces in his country most solidly represented by Saliq al-Mahdi, grandson of the fanatic who defeated Lord Gordon. Although Nimeiry has tried to reach a compromise with Mahdi and has welcomed him into the government, the relationship has been stormy. Mahdi

resigned in protest from the Central Committee of the Sudanese Socialist Union when the Sudan did not oppose Sadat's
peace policy. He has yet to come back into the fold and still
represents the perfect rallying point for forces in the country
bent on overthrowing the government.

A weak economy, constantly on the verge of bankruptcy, also
leaves Nimeiry performing an increasingly difficult balancing
act. The United States, in trying to keep Nimeiry's regime intact, has made the Sudan its number one aid recipient in Africa.
Other Western nations have followed the U.S. lead. Germany,
in addition to extending new loans, has forgiven some $220
million worth of old debts. Other nations, such as Japan, France,
the Netherlands, England, even Italy, are lending their support.

U.S. support for the Sudan gratifies the Saudis, but they also
want the United States to give aid to Somalia, whose Arab socialist government is supporting the ethnic Somali secessionists in
Ethiopia. The United States refuses for the same reason that it
will give no succor to Eritrean rebels in Ethiopia: it fears that
aid to such a breakaway movement could set a precedent for
redrawing borders all over Africa.

On top of their triumphs in the Horn, the Soviets scored
another breakthrough when a pro-Soviet junta took control of
the strategically situated nation of Afghanistan, in the northeastern corner of the triangle. Afghanistan, however, has shown
how vulnerable the Soviets are in their adventurism.

Just as in Ethiopia, the Soviet-sponsored regime in power is
opposed by grassroots guerrilla movements. But the Afghan
guerrillas are not nearly so self-destructively divided as those in
Ethiopia, and may need little help to bog down the Soviets in
an embarrassing Vietnam-style fiasco.

Thus, in just a few years, the United States has lost its biggest
investment in Africa to the Soviet Union, has seen radicals who
owe the United States nothing but resentment take over in
Iran, has lost to the Soviet sphere states on either side of the

Strait of Babel Mandeb, and has seen Soviet military might on
station grow to enormous proportions—not just in size but in
strategic shape as well.

The Soviet Game-Plan

The man behind this Soviet strategy is Admiral Sergei Ghorsh-
kov, who for the past twenty years has been commander in
chief of the Soviet navy. As might be expected from the besieg-
ers of Stalingrad, it is a strategy that puts logistic might above
flamboyant showings of the flag. In fact, much of the might of
the Soviet armada is to be found in its "commercial" fleet,
which has been growing at a much quicker rate than the
U.S.S.R.'s foreign trade would warrant. The Soviets now have
the world's largest fleet of liners and have ambitious expansion
plans.

So far this development has been largely the focus of commercial complaints. The Common Market's commissioner for
transportation, Richard Burke, complains that Soviet state buying power, along with cheap labor, is undermining Western
fleets. But it is also doing something else: it is proving to be of
enormous strategic significance in regions like the Persian Gulf.
Indeed, the Soviet emphasis on supply and logistics extends to
the character of its naval fleet proper. On the Indian Ocean one
is much more likely to encounter supply vessels prepared for
combat rather than combat vessels ferrying supplies. Alligator-
class supply ships have bombarded Eritrean guerrillas from
their moorings at Massawa.

NATO's secretary general, Dr. Joseph Luns, makes the obvious but too easily overlooked point that Soviet capabilities are
"the one accurate measure" of Soviet plans. What are those
plans? In his book *The Sea Power of the State,* Gorshkov puts
forth a number of doctrines of nuclear warfare, but beyond this
he also emphasizes the uses of military power short of nuclear

war. Specifically, he recommends a force capable of operating at long distances and able to influence political change in peacetime. Recent refugees from the Soviet Union say their navy is emphasizing ways of maintaining sailors' morale during prolonged stays abroad and of perfecting logistics and resupply.

Already, the Soviet fleet spends three times as many "ship days" in the Indian Ocean as do the U.S. ships. But during the current phase of their plans, the Soviets are still concentrating on supply and securing new bases, rather than on fleet-building. Aside from the major base on Socotra Island, they have established facilities in Yemen proper and on the island of Mauritius, and if the Eritreans ever cease to be a threat to them, bases can be expected on the Eritrean coast of Ethiopia. Soviet generals, Cuban troops, and massive amounts of Soviet weaponry have been involved in active operations in Ethiopia for more than a year. According to Gorshkov, such bases need not be used in order to be effective; merely by existing, they display "the economic and military power of a country beyond its borders." In addition to maintaining bases, the Soviets enjoy, from time to time, landing rights in Libya, Syria, and Iraq for its warplanes.

Soviet planners stress that a force on station is much more effective than a force that must be rushed to the scene. No matter how quickly new technology may permit such movements, an arriving force could well be confronting a fait accompli by the time it lands. "Right through the sixties the Mediterranean was an American lake," said one U.S. planner. "Then the 1973 Yom Kippur War broke out, and scores of Soviet surface ships poured in from the Black Sea. Then some twenty-five subs moved down from the Baltic, and now we must worry about the Red Sea becoming a Soviet lake."

The U.S. Response So Far

The Carter administration, alarmed by Soviet inroads, is planning to beef up U.S. naval presence in the Indian Ocean as one way of assuring the Saudis and Persian Gulf sheikdoms that the United States is committed to protecting their security. Right after the takeover of the U.S. embassy in Tehran in November 1979 and the taking of sixty American hostages, pressure in Congress became intense to fund a $2 billion Rapid Deployment Force. The special strike force of 110,000 men drawn from the 82nd and 101st Airborne divisions and elements of two Marine divisions would give the United States the means to intervene quickly, and in force, virtually anywhere in the world— and especially in the Middle East. It's a measure of how strained relations have become that the Saudis have been decidedly cool to such moves. Nonetheless, despite conciliatory Saudi gestures to Iran, South Yemen, and the Soviet Union, their interests still lie with the West and the United States, and Congress is likely to approve funding for an increased presence in the region. "We clearly need an increase in conventional strength directed at the problems of the Middle East and Asia," said Senator Richard Stone (D.-Fla.), chairman of the Near East Subcommittee of the Senate Foreign Relations Committee. And in the House, Representative Samuel S. Stratton (D.-N.Y.), the third-ranking Democrat and the acknowledged Mideast expert on the Armed Services Committee, predicted that Congress will "be kindly disposed to increasing the American presence out there."

Defense Secretary Harold Brown, during a late-February 1979 swing through the Middle East, promised more weapons for Saudi Arabia, Egypt, and other U.S. friends in the region. He said, on his return, "I went there to reassure our friends that the United States will take a more active role—militarily and in terms of economic development—in the region, and I believe they were assured." By July, a $1.2 billion military sales package had been put together, and so concerned was the administration over the deterioration of security in the area that it began to seem the deal would be brought off even if the Saudis failed to oblige congressional and administration demands that they lend more support to Egypt in its confrontation with the Arab world over peace with Israel. Indeed, there appears to be growing congressional awareness that the Saudis feel too insecure to choose sides between Sadat and the militant Arabs. Many in Congress, like Senator Frank Church (D.-Idaho), continue to overrate the Saudis' ability to lead the Arab world from what has long been the provincial back-country of the Arabs. But after Fahd's visit to Washington was canceled to avoid any appearance of Saudi association with a United States–sponsored deal between Israel and Egypt, the light slowly began to dawn. And when, after much hemming and hawing, the Saudis reneged on a promise to pay for Egypt's purchase of American-made jets, the reality of their political weakness began to be clear.

Sadat, for his part, says he is willing to take over the shah's role as policeman of the area, provided the United States supplies him with modern arms. But other Arabs are wary of Egypt's playing such a role, and the Egyptian army probably lacks much ability to intervene beyond neighboring Sudan or Libya.

Militarily, Egypt remains the one bright spot for the United States in the Middle East. Although there are many problems that make the country vulnerable, and though the relationship with Israel is explosive, Sadat and Carter have received each other in a mutually beneficial embrace. In 1979 the United States will give Egypt more than $1 billion in aid. The money will provide forward spin to Egypt's modernization efforts. New power plants, irrigation projects, investments in agribusiness, will all help the country onto the path of the twentieth century. The benefit for the United States: a hedge against a deteriorating position in the Middle East.

Egypt and Israel

Egypt's modernization efforts got off to a shaky start in 1974, when Sadat embarked on a course to reverse the years of economic stagnation of the Nasser regime. He introduced the open door policy, which was meant to draw foreign investors to Egypt by offering various tax benefits and exemptions. But foreigners did not clamor to get in, as had been expected. They were scared away by a dual exchange rate that worked to their disadvantage when they tried to repatriate profits. And then there was the labyrinthine Egyptian bureaucracy. The maze that was developed to thwart the British now confounds the Egyptians as well. Americans in particular have been reluctant to jump in with both feet. They have been especially discouraged by Egyptian customs laws, which permit the taxation of materials and equipment brought in to set up industry. Earlier this year top Egyptian officials met with businessmen and economists from all over the world. The Egyptians came away with a resolve to slash bureaucracy, simplify their customs laws, and eliminate contradictory regulations in order to appeal more to the foreign investor.

Renewed foreign investment, reinforced by massive aid from the West, in particular the United States, West Germany, the Netherlands, France, and England, has given Egypt a chance to start becoming productive on its own. Last year Egypt became a net exporter of oil, to the tune of $700 million, and receipts from the Suez Canal, tourism, and Egyptians working abroad have been steadily rising. There is also a greater drive now to improve the quality of Egyptian goods so that they will be competitive in Western markets.

Although much of Nasser's socialist bureaucracy remains in place, rigidly enforcing a plethora of socialist regulations still on the books, Sadat has by now managed to maneuver Egypt firmly into the U.S. camp, and is striving to achieve the American vision of peace in the Middle East through the treaty with Israel. Indeed, the uneasy peace that has been reached may be the most fragile time bomb ticking in the Middle East. Other countries have internal problems that could result in civil war or border conflict, but a collapse of the Egyptian-Israeli peace could lead to a conflagration that would spread beyond the borders of Egypt and Israel to involve almost the entire region.

If that happens, the spark could well come from Libya. It is not simply that Libyan President Muammar el-Qaddafi is almost continuously provocative himself. There is also the possibility of a pre-emptive strike against Libya by the Egyptians, because war with Libya would probably unite the Egyptian populace should it become restive because peace fails to bear its promised economic fruit.

In fact, despite Israel's history of pre-emptive strikes, and despite agonizing foot-dragging in Israel over Palestinian autonomy, the Arab states appear to pose more of a threat to the peace than do the Israelis. Arab shock at Camp David has been so severe that it has brought radical Palestinians together with Jordan's moderate King Hussein, and the Israelis believe that now that the initial accords have been signed, the fragile alliance of Iraq and Syria may well try to embarrass Egypt by provocative acts and subversion.

The radicals could do this in a number of ways. They could move Iraq's massive military might up to Syria's border with Israel, thus prompting a pre-emptive strike; or if this did not work, Syrian forces in Lebanon could move to put an end once and for all to the quasi-independent, still-armed Christian community, which holds an enclave from the outskirts of Beirut north to its working capital of Jounie. In that case, the Israelis would probably move north and make an amphibious landing at Jounie, intending to secure the enclave and the separate Christian strip that runs between Israel's northern border and the Litani River. Given the character of modern warfare, though, they could well end up not only with that territory but with a huge new captive population. Such a "victory" would hardly be a blessing, especially if it involved a rupture with Egypt; but for Iraq and Syria it could be even more disastrous, involving possible devastation of their armies, burgeoning industries, and perhaps even Iraq's oil fields.

The Israelis do believe that the United States has far overrated the Saudis as a political force and, consequently, their ability to moderate Arab opinion even if they wanted to. They realize that the numerically small and culturally backward Saudis are primarily an economic force, barely a political or military one outside their own borders. What is more, the Saudis, being deeply religious, have been unable to abide Camp David's skirting of the Jerusalem issue. Thus, one Camp David dividend widely discussed in U.S. defense circles—an anticommunist alliance of Israel, Egypt, and Saudi Arabia—appears highly unlikely. For now, it would seem the best the United States could hope for is a tacit alliance of Saudi money, U.S. arms, and Egyptian manpower. In fact, much of the rationale for such cooperation (mutually desired stability, resistance to the Soviets) still exists, but, as has been seen, it is working poorly, if at all.

The Iraqi Fuse

As if the face-off between the Iraqi-led radicals on the one hand and the Egyptians and Israelis on the other were not volatile enough, instability in Iraq renders the situation all the more dangerous. Leftist Iraq claimed to be pleased by the popular Iranian uprising against the shah's elite, but the revolution in

Iran has served only to stir up popular resentment against the country's own minority government. Now that the Shiites (also known as Shiahs) in Iran have triumphed against all the guns and ammunition of the shah, the Ayatollah Khomeini is encouraging the Shiites in Iraq to rise up, to resist the might of the Sunni minority, which controls the ruling Ba'ath Party. And it may not be difficult. There are approximately 5.5 million Shiites in Iraq, but only 2 million Sunnis. On the surface, this disproportion may not look too extreme. But the ruling Sunnis make up only 15 percent or so of the country's population. In fact, many of the Sunnis are not Arabs. They are Kurds, constantly at war with the Arab state. In recent years, Baghdad had largely defeated the Kurdish uprising of Mullah Mustafa al-Barzani, who began his career during World War II with the backing of the Soviets and then solicited Western sponsorship when radicals took over in Baghdad. (He died in the United States while in exile.) The Arabs were able to accomplish this by reaching a modus vivendi with the shah, whereby, in exchange for the Iraqis relinquishing claim to chiefly Arab-populated regions of the Shatt-al-Arab estuary surrounding Iran's largest port, Khorramshahr, the Iranians agreed to cease granting Barzani's Kurds free passage through Kurdish regions in Iran. But now the Iranians are said to have permitted Barzani's son to return to Iranian Kurdistan, from where he has proceeded to Iraqi Kurdistan to revive the insurgency. With their country in disarray, the Iranians have their own reasons to fear Kurdish separatism, just as they do separatist movements among the Baluchis and other such groups. But paradoxically, for this very reason they have a motive for helping the Kurds against the Iraqis. For one thing, such a move may appease Kurdish separatist sentiment in Iran. And, more important, Iran has been worried about Iraqi ambitions to regain control of Khuzistan, the Iranian province that contains almost all of Iran's onshore oil. The province is populated primarily by Arabs and is frequently called, by both Persians and Arabs, Arabistan, its former name. The Arabs in that quarter move with ease across the border on gunrunning missions.

Chances are the Iraqis neither intend nor have the nerve to grab the oil province. More likely, they are financing and arming the disaffected Arabs of the region merely to strengthen their key bargaining card in the power game with the new Iranian regime. In the meantime, however, the Arab-Persian animosity of four centuries, only recently quieted, is being rekindled. In the current mood of religious and ethnic revival that is gripping the Middle East, forces could be set in play that neither the Iraqi nor the Iranian government could control.

In an effort to consolidate its power base in this superheated political climate, the leadership in Baghdad has removed the heads of the various Shiite provinces and replaced them with Sunnis known to be loyal to the government. In the central Euphrates area, where most of the Shiite tribes are found, a state of near–civil war exists. Arrests and demonstrations have been reported in the Shiite towns of Karbala and An Najaf. In addition, Abdel Hussein Mashhadi, a prominent Shiite member of the Revolutionary Command Council, was removed from that body and also expelled from the Ba'ath Party. Mashhadi was the first prominent official to go in a purge being carried out by Iraqi strongman Saddam Hussein shortly after he became president of the country, replacing the long-time figurehead, Ahmed Hassan al-Bakr.

Though Hussein has proved expert at such deadly infighting, he and his ruling Sunni minority may now be cutting too severely their lines to other power bases. In the past, although they have ruled as a minority, they have done so while cultivating de facto alliances with powerful Kurds, Armenians, and Shiite Arabs willing to compromise their ethnic integrity. How well they can fare without such alliances is a proposition yet to be tested.

Mashhadi was dismissed because he was suspected of having

dealings with the Ayatollah Khomeini. But, expressed differ-
ently, it could be said that Mashhadi was a leading member of
the Iraqi ruling faction willing to see Iraq deal with Khomeini,
and his dismissal is a clear sign that Hussein's regime feels too
insecure to pursue such a partnership. Nor is Hussein's chari-
ness limited to the Iranians. Many of those expelled from government are widely believed to have had Libyan and other
radical connections, though just the opposite was claimed officially at the time of their dismissal.

For some time now the Iraqis have been trying to replace
Egypt as the center of the Arab world, but without much success, given the dominant position of Egypt in its confrontation
with the Arabs' nemesis, Israel, and the cultural pre-eminence
of Cairo in the Arab world. Often as not, in their efforts to outdo
all other Arabs in their opposition to Israel and thereby take the
lead, the Iraqis merely wound up adopting unworkable and
uncompromising positions that put them at the fringe rather
than at the center of the action. But when Sadat began bilateral
negotiations with Israel, the Iraqis saw their opportunity. They
abandoned their extremist posturing and took steps to bring
together Arabs of the left and right in opposition to Zionism.
They called a Baghdad conference at which the Camp David
accords were rejected and sanctions against Egypt were
mapped out. Later, after Egypt signed an initial accord with
Israel, Baghdad called a follow-up meeting. It again played a
moderating role and got eighteen Arab delegations to agree on
a more specific set of economic and political sanctions against
Cairo.

Iraq's moderating posture has won new, albeit uneasy,
friends. After a decade of hostility, Iraq and Syria announced
plans to unite. Although the union will probably never actually
take place, reciprocal terrorist attacks have been suspended.
The unity talks have stalled because of difficulties in reuniting
rival branches of the Ba'ath Party and because of Syria's lingering fear of being absorbed by richer and larger Iraq.

The Iraqis have even made peace with the conservative gulf state Arabs. Saudi Arabia is said to have signed an agreement with Iraq that includes technical and administrative exchanges as well as mutual cooperation on security. Iraq is now talking with Kuwait, which is also worried over unrest among the Shiites, about cooperation in linking electrical grids, forming a pan–Persian Gulf railway, and sharing Iraq's waters. Heavily armed by the Soviets, Iraq once threatened to invade Kuwait. But that danger, Kuwaitis believe, has been eliminated by the Iranian revolution.

Relations have improved with both Bahrain and the United Arab Emirates. Some Arab experts maintain that the Saudis and their gulf allies are so frightened by instability, however divinely inspired it may be, that they will almost certainly side with their old radical opponent in the event of confrontation with Iran.

Already Iraqi-Iranian tensions have revived wider Arab-Persian rivalries. Recently, the gulf Arabs resurrected their claims to three gulf islands of some military importance. Abu Musa, Tanb-e Bozorg, and Bani Tanb were seized by the shah when the British pulled out of the Persian Gulf in 1971. Although the action offended the Arabs greatly, they chose not to make an international claim for them. Now, however, they are doing so. In return, Iran has renewed its claim to Bahrain, the island-state in the Persian Gulf.

In addition to displaying their newly developed political skill, the Iraqis are also proving an economic force of considerable substance. They have both oil wealth and a relatively educated population to match. Oil export revenues are expected to reach $13 billion this year, and unlike Iran, whose reserves are rapidly dwindling, Iraq has more oil than it knows of. The reason: just as they did when their assets were nationalized in Mexico, the multinational oil companies took the exploration maps home with them when their assets were nationalized by Iraq. For years, the Iraqis have been trying, in effect, to rediscover oil deposits already found but undisclosed by the giants. However, Iraq is making new commercial alliances with European oil consumers, particularly France, and in today's oil-thirsty world it is unlikely that Iraq's enormous reserves will remain out of reach for long.

A conflict with either Iran or Israel could set back the solid economic gains the Iraqis have made by balanced investments of their oil revenues in industry, infrastructure, and agriculture. Even before the Iranian revolution, the Iraqi Ba'ath Party had started mending fences with its neighbors by ending its feud with Syria's Ba'athist ruling party and proposing the union of the two countries. As a result, Syria has reopened Iraq's oil pipeline outlet to the Mediterranean, and other economic ties are being strengthened.

Little real progress toward political unity is likely, however. After several years of stable rule under President Hafez al-Assad, Syria is slipping back into the insecure political climate that prevailed before Assad seized power. Previously, coups occurred with almost annual regularity.

But Syria is particularly in trouble now because of the challenge thrown up by Camp David. From a Western point of view, the risk for Egypt is all too apparent. But it has also cast the Arab radical world in disarray. The Iraqi-Syrian alliance was supposed to substitute for the Syrian-Egyptian alliance. It is a poor substitution. Quite beyond the fragility of the alliance (Syria's former alliances with Egypt were also fragile), the simple loss of Egypt as the most populous and most militarily effective ally has been a fundamentally shaking experience. The argument that Iraq can substitute for Egypt is so patently weak that any political power which must use it to paper over the truth is, perforce, skating out onto thin political ice. Because both the Syrian and Iraqi presses are tightly controlled, it is not easy to judge, but by now it is apparent that there has been a marked drop in popular confidence.

Iran

Picking up the pieces of Iran's economy, despite the euphoria of the Ayatollah Khomeini's revolution, will be extremely difficult. "The problems are very closely tied to the political situation, which is far from stabilized," observed a diplomat in Tehran.

What the diplomat referred to was the fundamental difference in goals between Prime Minister Mehdi Bazargan, a French-educated moderate who wanted to continue modernizing Iran's economy and to restore its links with the West before he resigned in November 1979, and the Islamic radicals around Khomeini, who would turn back the clock. Indeed, the months following the revolution have revealed a government that becomes more fragmented each day. Real authority eluded Bazargan, and it slowly slipped away from Khomeini himself. Members of the clergy serving the ayatollah created a sphere of power; the Islamic Revolutionary Committees made up another sphere. The committees, however, so extended their own power that even Khomeini himself would have difficulty dislodging them if he chose to do so. The various ethnic minorities within the country are also becoming spheres of power.

There's no way of predicting with certainty what economic structure will emerge in Iran. However, Khomeini's heavy support from the bazaar merchants who financed his movement seem to assure a place for small business, while from the beginning large industries have appeared to be targets for government take-over. And, in fact, by July of 1979 all major banks, insurance companies, steel mills, and auto plants had been nationalized.

"Our priority is meeting our foreign obligations," said former Finance Minister Ali Ardalan. That will require processing foreign bills, which will absorb up to half of Iran's $10 billion in international reserves. But the central bank, lacking a governor or deputy governors, is still virtually paralyzed by a strike committee that will not allow department heads to act without its consent.

Resumption of crude-oil exports, to the levels of 6 million barrels a day they were at under the shah, is highly unlikely and contrary to the new regime's philosophy, which mandates maximum conservation. Beyond that lies the prickly political issue of marketing the oil, which until December 1978 was sold mainly to a British–United States–French consortium. There was strong pressure to by-pass the consortium as a legacy of Western imperialism, and it was by-passed. Senior officials of the National Iranian Oil Company say they will sell to the highest bidder—a prospect that stirs some skepticism. "They're a bit naïve to suppose they can sell their oil on the spot market for long," said one Tehran observer when the new policy was outlined. Japan, highly dependent on Iranian oil, was eager to buy, but after an initial scramble in a market stretched tight by the revolution, buyers became wary of Iran's reliability as a supplier. And despite their aggressive posture, the Iranians began to ease the price somewhat, and to favor medium-term contracts.

U.S. companies with investments and uncompleted engineering contracts in Iran, meanwhile, are mostly watching and waiting. The Du Pont Company, which has the biggest direct U.S. investment in Iran, says its minority-owned fibers plant is mostly shut down but is being manned by an Iranian maintenance crew. The Ralph M. Parsons Company, a major engineering company headquartered in Pasadena, California, withdrew American personnel from a copper mine and gas-gathering system that it was working on. But it is optimistic that the projects will be completed because they will earn export income. Even if Iran stopped payments, according to President Otha C. Roddey, Parsons has "no exposure," because all equipment is owned by local subcontractors. In addition, the company "controls" enough construction material, paid for but not delivered, so that it could recover all sums owed it.

But a Midwest leasing company says it has $4 million worth of equipment still in Iran. "It hasn't been expropriated," said the company president. "The lessee is saying, 'We'll pay you.' But the banks are closed."

These uncertainties will not be cleared up until someone is able to consolidate his authority. But even if he succeeds in doing that, it will be only a first step.

If a moderate Bazargan-type can overcome continuous humiliations and somehow muddle through, the Iran that will emerge in three or four years will probably be more inclined to the West and less vulnerable to radical influence because the middle class that Bazargan had enfranchised are Western trained and used to dealing with the West. This is possible because Khomeini is not overly opposed to the middle class. Also, the masses that love Khomeini were also fond of Bazargan —even though he chided them for lack of discipline and their revered mullah for meddling and inconsistency. However, Khomeini is afraid of the sectarian middle class, especially that segment on the left. The danger is that in using his vigilante Komitehs to keep the middle class in line, Khomeini may so weaken the middle class–staffed central government that even if the professionals do not rise in revolt, the feeble government will prove incapable of controlling separatist Baluchis, Azerbaijanis, Kurds, Turkomans, and Arabs. And if that happens, the power vacuum could destroy the region's last vestiges of prudence and reason.

The Islamic Resurgence

The Soviet threat is only one of the dangers to the United States and to friendly governments in the Middle East. Although Iran may once again become a reasonably stable Islamic republic and a reliable oil supplier, it is still going through a dangerous radical phase, during which it is emitting political and religious shock waves. They are bound to create new instability in the region.

Probably the greatest danger posed by the Muslim resurgence is not any inherent tendency it has to radicalism or the Soviet line but its unpredictability. Events from Kabul to Khartoum may make it seem directed against the United States, but when Shiite Muslims in Afghanistan kidnaped the U.S. ambassador, they were not pro- but anti-Soviet. And the country currently reckoned most likely to be infected by Iran's Shiite unrest is Sunni-ruled, mostly Shiite Iraq. Iraq was not in the American camp to begin with; in fact, it is already as markedly radical as it can be without joining the Soviet camp. Nonetheless, it is impossible to gainsay the potential danger posed by the Muslim resurgence. Although the movement now is a weapon in no one's arsenal, it is as threatening as a drum of gasoline rolling loose on a street under siege. Without anyone's intention it could trigger a conflagration.

Signs of a fervid religious and ethnic revival are everywhere. In Turkey, battling leftists and rightists are divided as much by religion as politics—with the rightists being Sunni, and the leftists, members of the Shiite sect. In Lebanon, dissident Shiites recently hijacked an airplane to protest the mysterious disappearance of an important religious leader, Musa Sadr, in Libya. Sadr inspired and organized the export to Iran of the tapes recorded by Khomeini that fired the revolution.

And on the day Khomeini's movement installed Mehdi Bazargan in power, wildly shouting Sudanese marched on Khartoum's U.S. embassy in a procession reminiscent of one led by the Mahdi who had had Lord Gordon beheaded, and whose grandson, Saliq al-Mahdi, presents a serious Muslim challenge to the United States–backed regime of President Jaafer al-Nimeiry.

Iranian officials, flushed with the success of the Ayatollah Khomeini's Islamic revolution, are already denouncing the "oppressive" Saudi monarchy and are predicting a possible Islamic uprising in Egypt. But the repercussions from Iran could also shake radical governments. Iraqi strongman Saddam Hussein sees the outburst in Iran as a direct threat to his militant Ba'ath socialist state.

A sect given to mysticism, fanaticism, self-flagellation, and periods of deep mourning over the martyrdom of the seventh-century Imam Hussein, the Shiites who predominate among Iran's Persians also predominate among Iraq's Arabs. However, Hussein is a Sunni, and his Ba'ath Party is overwhelmingly controlled by the more traditional Sunni sect of Islam. Curiously enough, the Ba'ath Party in Syria, with which Iraqi Ba'athists long feuded and have only recently made hasty peace, represents precisely the opposite situation. The Syrian Ba'ath Party is dominated by President Hafez al-Assad's Shiite Alewites, and most Syrians are Sunni. Recently a new Sunni religious group managed to assemble a group of Alewite officer cadets in an auditorium, where grenades were tossed into their midst.

In Saudi Arabia Shiite Muslims, mostly in the eastern oil-producing provinces of Saudi Arabia, celebrated the Iranian revolution by putting up posters of the Ayatollah Khomeini. But they were a minority, and it was initially hoped that the Muslim resurgence would have slight impact in mostly Sunni Saudi Arabia, which was already a strict Islamic state. The Saudi royal family has close ties with religious leaders, who must approve the selection of the king, and with the puritanical Bedouin tribes that supply the riflemen for the national guard. But simple fear of Iran has by itself already heavily influenced Saudi relations, particularly with the United States, and, as we have seen, there have been reports of contacts between Saudi dissidents and Khomeini's lieutenants, including at least one reported coup attempt.

Even in Cairo more and more cosmopolitan women are wearing modest Islamic garb, and tape recordings of sermons by a blind preacher called Abdel Hamid Kishk are the latest rage. President Anwar el-Sadat, who has been the object of assassination attempts by religious zealots, is giving increasing attention to religious affairs even as he watches that the once-dangerous Muslim Brotherhood does not step out of line.

The Iranian revolution as a religious force will be difficult to export to Egypt. Within Islam, Egypt is distanced from Iran by the great schism between the Sunnis, who predominate in most Islamic countries, and the Shiites of the Ayatollah Khomeini, who are the majority only in Iran and Iraq. By contrast with Iran, where the mullahs have traditionally played the role of protectors of the faithful against the rulers, in Egypt the clergy are closely tied to the government. And unlike the shah, who showed little respect for religion and openly antagonized the mullahs, President Sadat is a devout Muslim and an astute politician, who loses no opportunity to be photographed at prayer. The Islamic group that could give Sadat trouble is the right-wing Muslim Brotherhood. But the brotherhood is believed to be numerically weak, though Sadat allows some factions to operate in order to counter Egyptian leftists. Very often Sadat mutes rambunctious holy men who oppose him by appointing them to high office.

Nonetheless, for economic reasons Egypt is vulnerable to the unsettling impact of the Iranian turmoil. Impoverished and crowded, it is no longer able to feed itself. And migrants streaming from rural villages into sprawling Cairo and other cities are creating urban chaos. There are signs of a modest pickup in investment following a freeze that businessmen, foreign and domestic, imposed on themselves while they waited to see the impact of the Arab boycott of Egypt. But the boycott is not dead, and it has its own religious rationale—return of Muslim East Jerusalem. If the Egyptians do not see the promised economic fruits of peace, their discontent could easily take a religious focus. Indeed, much of the Mideast ferment that is described as religious reflects deep economic tensions, too.

Thus, religious turmoil clearly threatens U.S. foes as well as friends. To some extent the result of the present upheaval will depend on how the West plays its advantages and covers its bets. As the Muslim revival builds apace, however, there are more than enough bets to cover.

Energy Policy

NOWHERE IS THE IMPACT of the decline of U.S. power—and the crisis of American leadership—more evident than in the crucial area of energy. In the years since OPEC grabbed control of the world oil market and began to exact the pleasures of monopoly, American policy-makers have been living in a fool's paradise, substituting rhetoric for action. Massive hikes in the price of oil tipped the world into recession twice in the 1970s. And the outlook for the decade ahead is even worse than the dark days of 1974–1975, when the global economy was pushed by OPEC into the worst recession since the Great Depression. At that time, the price of oil was raised a mammoth 400 percent. Now, however, not only is the oil price skyrocketing, but the supply of the vital energy source is suddenly being limited through political manipulation and, even more important, drastic declines in world reserves. The end of the petroleum age is upon us, and unless a remedy is found fast, this will surely curb the growth of all industrial nations in the 1980s, increase unemployment and inflation, and give rise to terrible social and political pressures that may threaten pluralistic democracies around the world.

Ironically, the American response to the oil crisis of the late 1970s was not all that different from the reaction to the gas lines of 1974. At that time, Washington politicians inveighed against OPEC for its greed, consumers refused to believe the oil crisis was real and blamed it all on big oil companies, and energy experts advocated making the United States self-sufficient in fuel. But once the gas lines disappeared, so did the burst of concern and activity. When the gas lines reappeared in the spring of 1979, the repetition of events was astounding: the 60 percent jump in oil prices by OPEC, plus lower oil production due to the Iranian collapse, produced a second rush of urgency about energy, and the very same issues and policies debated in 1974 were again put back on the American political agenda. Repeating history, the evaporation of concern that came with the disappearance of the gas lines in 1974 also occurred five years later. The emergency oil program proposed by President Carter in the summer was whittled down by Congress during the winter. And the strategic petroleum reserve authorized by Congress in 1975, after the Arab oil embargo, to protect the nation against interruptions in foreign supplies began to dry up as the administration in 1979 suspended purchases for fear of driving up world prices.

Unfortunately, the five-year gap between oil crises may simply have been the eye of a hurricane for the United States. Beneath the furor over OPEC challenges on the price front, the world's oil reserves, which had been rising for decades, quietly began declining, and production growth started to slow down. For the first time in the history of the United States, a drilling boom failed to turn up any major new reserves to alleviate the oil shortage, thus casting doubt on whether decontrol of crude-oil prices, one of the few policies actually put into effect by the United States, will really work to expand domestic supplies. Overseas, the likelihood of further discoveries of massive oil reserves is now doubtful, and even if the Saudis end their political capping of oil production for the West and run their wells at top speed, the energy crisis will only be postponed from the 1980s to the 1990s. Through all of this, Washington continues to fail to face the critical energy problem and come up with practical solutions for the country. The synthetic-fuel plants proposed in 1974 would have been built by 1979 had the proper incentives been offered by the federal government. And the congressional thrust drastically to cut back synfuels even now promises that

America will still be dependent on foreign oil when the new oil crisis hits some years down the road.

World Reserves Fall

No one knows when it happened, but sometime in the mid 1970s the total of the world's proven, commercially recoverable oil reserves appear to have peaked at about 675 billion barrels and began to fall. They fell to the 652 billion mark at the beginning of 1979, and are still on their way down. This is the first time in the present century that world reserves have not been rising, and this basic change in the global energy position underlies the oil crises of the 1970s and the coming problems of the 1980s. Of course, high oil prices could temporarily boost the reserve total by making it profitable for oil companies to produce in marginal fields. And the Saudis might increase their exploration and add several dozen billion barrels of oil to the numbers, but the trend is clear and alarming: for the first time since oil became a major source of energy, the world's factories, fleets of cars, and electricity plants are burning up oil faster than it is being discovered.

In the 1960s, drillers found enough oil every year to provide for an annual world consumption of 12 billion barrels and add another 24 billion each year to the total known reserves. Now, however, with consumption running at a higher level of 20 billion barrels a year, the annual rate of discovery is running at only 14 billion barrels, so 6 billion barrels are actually being subtracted from world reserves every year.

If this trend continues, an energy crunch of enormous proportions will hit the United States and the rest of the world sometime in the 1980s. World demand is currently increasing at a 3 percent annual rate. The continuation of such an increase in demand would call for nearly 73 million barrels per day by 1985, compared with just 62 million barrels daily produced in

How the U.S. is running out of oil

Companies spend more on exploration...

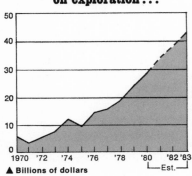

▲ Billions of dollars

... but find less new oil...

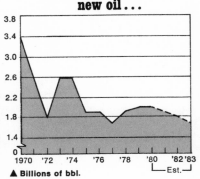

▲ Billions of bbl.

... drill many more domestic wells...

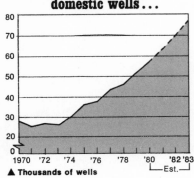

▲ Thousands of wells

... so total U.S. oil reserves decline

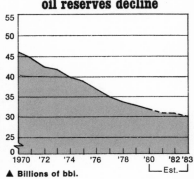

▲ Billions of bbl.

Data: American Petroleum Institute,
Chase Manhattan Bank

1979. But very little of this extra oil is likely to be produced. Crude-oil production is running well below the 3 percent demand rate, and by 1985 it will probably rise to only 66 million barrels daily—for an average increase of only 1 percent over the 1979 production and well below the 7 percent annual growth of the 1960s and early 1970s. By 1990, crude-oil output will probably peak out at only 70 million barrels per day and begin a long decline that lasts into the twenty-first century.

At the moment there are few prospects that this trend can be reversed. The simple reason is that the biggest accumulations of oil have probably been located already. "The amount of reserves we discover is not likely to be at the historical rate," said Arthur J. Warner, an analyst at the Energy Department. "The key is finding great fields, and most people doubt that we will find many more." One measure of the probability of increasing oil reserves is the discovery rate in drilling—and that has been falling for years. David Root, a resource analyst at the U.S. Geological Survey, notes that the discovery rate, or the number of barrels found per exploratory well, has been dropping for three decades. Moreover, despite the much higher oil prices, which have allowed companies to explore further offshore and at deeper depths, Root doesn't see the opening up of any more great oil reservoirs. The oil companies, he explained, "have already gone to places about as hideous as you can imagine."

A key factor in the oil equation for the 1980s is the looming switch of the Soviet Union from oil exporter to oil importer. Twice, in 1977 and again in 1979, the Central Intelligence Agency published reports predicting that the Soviet Union would become a net importer of oil by the early 1980s. Although the 1977 report was repudiated by both the Soviet Union and the major U.S. oil companies, it is now clear that the CIA was right on target. In the summer of 1979, the Soviet Union told its eastern European COMECON allies that it will not increase its oil exports to them any further and that any additional supplies in the decade ahead will have to be met through OPEC or other oil-exporting countries. Lubomir Strougal, the premier of Czechoslovakia, became the first senior eastern European official to say publicly that the Soviet Union is not going to increase its oil shipments in the new five-year COMECON plan, which begins in 1981. The Soviet decision will send eastern Europe into the Western oil markets, bidding for increasingly scarcer supplies of oil and sending prices ever higher.

For its part, the Soviet Union will also be entering the oil markets by the early 1980s. The CIA believes that nearly all of the country's oil fields are declining, except those in western Siberia. But even there, the huge Samotlor field, which provides half of the Soviet oil output, may be nearing its peak and may start to decline by 1981. By 1982, the Soviet Union could be importing 700,000 barrels of oil a day, and that figure will be substantially higher as the decade wears on. That would have tremendous consequences, not only for the oil market and the prices the United States would have to pay for its imported energy, but for Mideast politics as well.

The political competition between America and Russia now going on within the major OPEC producers in the Middle East will take on a much more vital economic meaning once the Soviet Union becomes dependent on foreign sources of oil for its own economic well-being. Even now there are rumors of Soviet oil sales to Saudi Arabia, and swaps of gold for oil are being discussed in major European capitals. The Saudis' desire to move some of their petromoney out of dollars into a harder investment vehicle while protecting their political flanks on the left at home can be met if they make a deal with the Soviet Union that would promise gold and stability.

At the moment, the Soviet Union remains the largest producer of oil in the world and has averaged about 11 million barrels per day in recent years. It exports 3 million barrels daily, with about 1 million going to the West and the rest to COMECON. Oil is the largest hard currency foreign exchange earner for the Soviet Union; without it, the country could not import the huge amounts of grain and machinery it needs to survive and grow. Oil and gas exports make up nearly 50 percent of hard currency export receipts, and in 1978 that came to nearly $5.5 billion.

Already, there are signs that Soviet oil production may have already peaked out. In April 1979, oil production hit a new high of 11.73 million barrels a day, but this dropped to 11.35 in May and continued downward. Output for the first five months of 1979 were about 6 million tons below target. During the entire decade of the seventies, the annual rate of increase in oil production was cut in half, from 8 percent to only 4 percent. The CIA believes that Soviet oil output can fall to 9.5 million barrels per day by 1985 if the trend is not reversed, and this can occur even if the Soviets embark on a major conservation program. The problem for the Russians is that they have neglected exploration while emphasizing heavy development of existing fields. Those fields in the Caspian and Ural-Volga regions are relatively shallow and accessible, and concentration on these areas has left the Soviet Union years behind in developing the proper technology for producing oil in more inhospitable areas. Until recently, there had been little incentive to develop sophisticated methods and equipment, and now only the United States has the know-how.

For its part, the United States has used its know-how to an incredible extent, in the last five years of the seventies, in a drilling boom unmatched in its history. Between 1973 and 1979, the number of wells drilled annually doubled to 50,000 as oil men saw the price of new-found oil zoom from $3.50 a barrel to the world level of $20 to $30. Unfortunately, for the United States all this drilling has produced very little new oil, and for the first time in 200 years, the lure of higher prices has not brought greater amounts of oil on stream. The decline in U.S. reserves and production that this drilling failure suggests means that for the 1980s the Soviet Union will begin to drag on the

international oil market, and America's already heavy dependence on foreign energy sources is likely to worsen.

The numbers showing a decline in U.S. oil output are already
staggering. Between 1975 and 1979, an average of 1.8 billion
barrels was discovered annually, well below the 1973 level of 2.6
billion. And even with the addition of 1.2 billion barrels a day
of new oil from Alaska, which began flowing in 1977, the present
domestic production rate of 10.2 million barrels daily is below
the pre-1973 embargo level. During this period, U.S. oil reserves
fell a whopping 20 percent, to 33.6 billion barrels. More and
more, the United States resembles the end of a played-out oil
field. "The easy oil has been found," said William Fisher, director of the Bureau of Economic Geology of the University of
Texas.

Behind the dramatic drop in U.S. oil reserves are the oil men's
dashed hopes of opening up major new offshore fields. In the
early 1970s, many oil men thought such fields held large new
pockets of crude. Drawn by much higher oil prices for new-
found crude, oil drillers looked hungrily at the outer continental shelf, or OCS, in the Gulf of Mexico, off the East Coast of the
United States, and off the shores of Alaska. Before 1973, almost
all of the 2.5 million oil wells drilled (more than four times as
many as those drilled by the rest of the noncommunist nations
combined) were put down into the shallow reservoirs onshore
or beneath the shallow waters of the Gulf of Mexico. But with
the massive hike in oil prices after the Arab oil embargo, the oil
held in the OCS, which in the past had been uneconomical to
develop, now seemed profitable. "The OCS was the great white
hope," remembered Lewis A. Ramsey, executive vice-president of Gulf Oil Exploration and Production Company.

That hope, of course, has been totally unfulfilled. Oil companies paid $1.1 billion in 1976 for rights to drill in the Baltimore
Canyon, off New Jersey, in the hope of finding a new oil bo-
nanza. But after months of drilling, the wells proved dry, and

the industry no longer expects to find any major commercial reserves there now. Earlier, a little-known exploration effort was made just off the Florida coast, on the so-called Destin Dome, and oil companies paid even more for the right to strike oil in the dome, one of the largest, most promising geological structures in North America. Had they succeeded, the Geological Society estimates that the Destin Dome's reserves would have equaled the 10 billion barrels found at Prudhoe Bay, Alaska. But unfortunately, the entire dome was bone dry. "OCS has been a bitter failure," admitted a top Exxon Corporation exploration executive, for a company that has spent about $2 billion on OCS leases and drilling since 1973 without much success.

That miserable record on drilling is giving second thoughts to a few people in Congress who voted for decontrol on the assumption that it would lead to higher oil production in the United States. "We have to ask the question 'What will we get for our money if we decontrol?' " said one Senate Energy Committee aide. If the government continues the decontrol program begun in June 1979, domestic oil prices should rise from a current average of $13.40 to the world price level by 1981. That level stood at about $23 in the fall of 1979, and it would almost certainly be near $30 per barrel by 1981. Such a price hike would pump a huge $60 billion (after normal taxes) into the oil industry's coffers between now and 1985, assuming Congress does not pass a special windfall profits tax on the new income.

The key question in Washington and elsewhere is how much of that would be reinvested in drilling and just what kind of return on increased oil production would result? Hardly any oil industry people are willing to admit that greater profits may not produce higher U.S. oil reserves. And when Robert W. Baldwin, the president of the Gulf Refining and Marketing Company, said in May 1979 that decontrolling U.S. oil prices would not prevent the continuing fall of production, he caused a tremendous uproar. "He came as close as anybody to singlehandedly losing decontrol," said one oil company's public relations official.

Still, Baldwin's brave comment probably reflects a growing belief within the oil industry that the magical effect higher prices once had on greater drilling and higher production will never work nearly as well in the future as it did in the past. With this in mind, the industry is now much more cautious as a whole in projecting production benefits from the decontrol of prices. The American Petroleum Institute estimates that with the 60 percent windfall profits tax Congress is likely to vote, decontrol may result in an extra 500,000 barrels per day of incremental production by 1985. But with the normal 4 percent annual decline in production without decontrol, that added oil could not stop total U.S. oil production from falling from the current 10.2 million barrels daily to 8.5 million by 1985. And even if, by some political miracle, Congress decided not to pass any windfall profits tax at all on the oil companies, oil men say that the additional 1.5 million barrels per day that might be produced would still not prevent a small overall production decline by 1985.*

In the end, decontrol may have its greatest impact on the tertiary oil produced in the United States—oil produced through the use of special processes, such as flushing crude with chemicals. Nearly 70 percent of all the oil found in the country falls into this category and cannot be produced conventionally. At present, the special processes cannot be used either economically or effectively. But decontrol may change the mathematics on tertiary oil to the point where oil men can turn a profit. If decontrol can cut into the 70 percent now excluded from total U.S. reserves by only 10 percentage points, that would raise the total U.S. reserve by 40 billion barrels, doubling current estimates. Yet the key is economics.

*The Decline of U.S. Power went to press before Congress voted on the windfall profits tax.

Synthetic-Fuels Disaster

The search for an economic alternative to pumping crude oil from the ground remains at the heart of the new push for synthetic fuels. Back in 1974, the last time the country was hit by an oil crisis, attention was quickly focused on alternatives to imported oil and a means of replenishing declining domestic reserves. Nuclear power and coal were then the darlings of the Nixon and Ford administrations, which considered them the dynamic duo that could make America self-sufficient in energy by the end of the 1980s.

Both have proved to be bitter disappointments. Nuclear power was once, back in the 1950s and 1960s, thought to be the answer to the problem of providing cheap, clean fuel. The earliest cost estimates right after World War II had nuclear plants producing electricity at a fraction of the cost of conventional power plant production. But that was before the construction delays, waste-processing problems, and inflationary pressures began to work their havoc. Costs were sent zooming to the point where nearly all of nuclear power's earlier economies relative to other fuels were eliminated. Reactor orders began to decline sharply from a peak of forty-one in 1973 to absolutely zero in 1978. More than twenty orders were canceled between 1975 and 1979. And that was well before the near-catastrophe at the Three Mile Island nuclear reactor in Pennsylvania in March 1979. To an incredible degree, that single accident, completely unforeseen by both the nuclear-power industry and the government regulatory bodies, has undermined public confidence in the safety of nuclear power and the competence of the private utilities in operating them.

There are seventy-two operating nuclear reactors on line right now, with about ninety-one additional reactors in various stages of completion. Even if the plants scheduled for start-up by 1985 are completed on time, total U.S. atomic capacity will peak at about 100,000 megawatts—or half what the Atomic Energy Commission had earlier projected for the mid 1980s. Instead of accounting for 12.7 percent of the nation's energy needs in 1985, as once predicted, nuclear power will account for only 7.2 percent. After first defaulting on promises of cheap energy, the nuclear-power industry now seems to have defaulted on promises of safety. It remains to be seen whether it can retrieve the initiative it held in the boom decades before the 1970s and go on to supply a major component of America's energy needs.

Coal has run into similar problems along the way to becoming the panacea for the United States' energy woes. The country controls nearly 20 percent of the world's huge coal deposits (which could last 600 years for the United States at present consumption rates), yet the coal industry has not yet been able to capitalize on the enormous hike in energy prices since 1974. Safety problems in the eastern coal mines and environmental problems from strip mining in the West have markedly slowed the expansion of coal production. But it is the major environmental problem attendant on burning coal directly into the air that has done the most to curb any dramatic expansion of this fuel as a replacement for imported oil. Total coal production is expected to hit 725 million tons in 1979, up 22.5 percent from 1973 but rising far too slowly to reach the goal of 1.5 billion tons by 1985 that the industry set back in 1974, after the oil embargo.

It is precisely because of the disappointments with nuclear power and coal that Washington policy-makers are now enthusiastic about the notion of building a huge new industry to produce oil and gas synthetically from coal and shale. Within weeks in the summer of 1979, right after the gas lines appeared for the second time in America, a blitz of synfuel-energy legislation hit Congress, calling for government funding, guarantees, and tax incentives for synthetic fuels.

In his July 15 address on energy, President Carter seized on the groundswell of public anger about the gas lines to rally the country behind his energy program based on synthetic fuels.

The President proposed the creation of an Energy Security Corporation, which would direct the investment of $88 billion to create the equivalent of 2.5 million barrels of daily oil production by 1990 through the development of various nonconventional sources—especially synthetic fuels. The corporation would finance such projects by making direct loans as well as loan guarantees, and by investing directly in a limited number of plants. It would also guarantee their prices.

The Carter message was reminiscent in style and spirit of Nixon's attempt to launch Project Independence years earlier. It tried to capture the same American spirit that supported a $35 billion project to land men on the moon. And, indeed, many major energy users were wholly caught up in it at first. "It [the synthetic-fuels program] is the only salvation for this country," said Henry E. Miller, assistant vice-president at Armco, Incorporated. And William W. Finley, Jr., a vice-president of Gulf Oil Corporation, insisted, "We should have started this program years ago."

Actually, most energy companies did start years ago. Of course, as far back as World War II, the Lurgi process was used to convert coal into oil for Hitler's military. But since the early 1970s, nearly every major oil company and natural-gas transmission line company has been researching ways of turning coal and shale into oil and gas. Within months after the 1973 Arab oil embargo, dozens of pilot and even commercial synfuel projects were announced. Among the more promising were four oil-shale plants undertaken by such major U.S. oil companies as Occidental Petroleum, Union Oil, Atlantic Richfield, and Indiana Standard. Each plant was supposed to produce at least 45,000 barrels per day of refined oil. When Gulf and Indiana Standard spent $210 million for the first federal oil-shale lease in early 1974, it looked as though a new synfuel-energy industry was beginning to take form.

In addition, gas companies undertook their own commercial synfuel projects, each designed to produce an amount of gas roughly equal to the energy output of the shale plants. The most advanced plans were those of Texas Eastern, El Paso, and American Natural Resources.

All of these plants were supposed to have come on stream by 1980 or before. If they had, the United States would have had a synthetic-fuel industry capable of producing the equivalent of 365,000 barrels of oil a day—roughly half of the nation's oil shortfall at its worst point in 1979. Unfortunately, not one of the plants is operating. And although most are still in some phase of development, none is expected to be producing commercial quantities of oil or gas until sometime in the mid 1980s, at best. In fact, the only synfuel projects actually to come on stream are two plants built by U.S. oil companies and Canadian corporations to produce oil from the vast deposits of tar sands in Alberta, and the projects are very limited in scope.

The U.S. projects have languished because the early cost estimates for synfuels proved to be totally unrealistic. At the same time, prices of imported crude oil, which synfuels were intended to displace, stabilized after the oil embargo for about five years, until 1979.

The cost projections for oil from shale have climbed steadily. In 1972, according to Edward W. Merrow of the Rand Corporation, shale oil was considered profitable at $6.60 a barrel, which at that time was three times the price of imported oil. When foreign oil jumped to $12 by 1975, the projections for shale oil's cost climbed to about $21, and now that shale price has climbed to about $26 to $30 a barrel by many estimates—still above the world oil price, although the gap is narrowing.

The same inflation crippled the coal-gas projects. In March 1979, Texas Eastern and its partner, the Pacific Lighting and Power Company, canceled plans on which they had been working since 1973 to build a commercial-sized coal-gasification plant near Farmington, New Mexico. At the time they had announced the project, they expected that it would cost $400 million and produce gas priced at the equivalent of $7.50 a barrel of oil. By 1977, costs had risen to $1.3 billion and $20 a barrel. Today, coal-gasification cost estimates hover around $30 a barrel.

Even a continuation of price increases by OPEC by no means resolves the cost uncertainties and enormous commercial risks of synfuel plants. Indeed, most experts believe that the plants cannot be built on a large scale without government supports, such as guaranteed markets and prices for the oil, and substantial tax incentives. "There's no way industry will do it on its own, but it's the right thing for the nation to do," said Robert F. Meeker, vice-president in charge of commercial energy development for TRW, Incorporated, which is a sponsor for an experimental project on coal gasification.

Until now that public support has been missing. The new factor that may finally get synthetic fuels on their way is that proposals for governmental assistance are gaining wider support, including that of big users of energy, who will ultimately foot the bill. "If we don't produce synthetic fuels, the cost of petroleum will have no limit," forecasted H. J. Meany, president of Norris Industries, Incorporated, a Los Angeles metalworking company.

But even with government support, the overwhelming consensus among energy experts is that synfuels will be no cure-all. At the very best, they say, a huge program might result in the construction by 1990 of a synfuel industry capable of producing the equivalent of 2 million barrels of oil a day, about 20 percent of the nation's present oil production. Based on the estimated capital costs of the commercial-sized oil-shale, coal-gasification, and coal-liquefaction plants that are now being planned, construction of such an industry would involve $60 billion in capital in current dollars, roughly double the amount spent last year on all plant construction.

But other obstacles are far more constraining than capital, which could be raised quite easily—and profitably—by investment bankers, given the appropriate government guarantees.

The leaders in synfuels

Project sponsor	Location	Cost (millions of dollars)	Production (thousands of bbl. per day)	Cost per bbl.	Status
Oil shale					
Occidental Petroleum	Colorado	$900	50	$20	Under construction for operation by 1985
Union Oil	Colorado	780	54	24	First phase awaiting government subsidy
Gulf/Standard (Ind.)	Colorado	NA	200	25	One pilot plant under way, another planned
ARCO/TOSCO	Colorado	1,300	45	25	Awaiting tax incentives
Coal gasification*					
American Natural Resources Group	N. Dakota	1,100	22	28	Awaiting government approval of tariffs
El Paso Co.	New Mexico	600	13	30	Delayed by lease, water rights problems
Coal liquefaction					
Gulf Oil (Energy Dept.)	W. Virginia	700	20	30	In design, planned completion by 1985
Exxon (Energy Dept., others)	Texas	1,700	30	30	$240 million pilot plant starts in 1980
Ashland (Energy Dept., others)	Kentucky	292	2	NA	Pilot plant begins this year
Tar sands					
Sun Co.	Alberta	480	58	10	Operating since 1967
Syncrude Canada Ltd.	Alberta	2,000	130	15	Begins operation this year

Data: BW estimates NA = not available *Production based on oil equivalent of gas

Courtesy of Business Week

The most menacing problem is the environmental impact that a major synfuel program would have in western states that contain enough coal and shale to support the plants. Replacing just 10 percent of the nation's oil production with synthetic fuels could require new mining capacity equal to half of today's U.S. coal production. The in situ processing of shale could preclude heavy mining, but environmentalists fear the conversion plants would mean heavy strip mining.

The projects would also consume enormous quantities of water, a commodity as precious to Westerners as energy is to the entire country. Synfuel plants consume about four times as much water as the amount of oil they produce. Thus, getting water rights could be a serious political problem.

Beyond that, a number of economists fear that an extensive effort to build synthetic-fuel plants would strain the capacity of the construction industry to provide enough engineers, heavy equipment, and skilled labor. That could force construction costs into an upward spiral much like the one that wrecked synfuel economics and halted progress on so many projects in the mid 1970s. "Within six to eight months of the start-up of a large-scale construction program, you are likely to run head-on into manpower problems," predicted D. Quinn Mills, professor of business administration at the Harvard Business School.

Despite such obstacles, many advocates argue that synfuels may prove to be more important as a psychological weapon against the power of OPEC than as a new source of oil. They suggest that if it demonstrates to the oil-producing nations that the United States is indeed determined to lessen its dependence on imports, a huge synfuel program could discourage OPEC from raising prices so rapidly. Considering that the United States now pays $60 billion annually for foreign oil, that deterrent may prove to be synthetic oil's greatest potential.

The search for a single, magical solution to counter what President Carter called the "excessive dependence on OPEC" has probably been the greatest obstacle in the country's finding a policy to counter the increasing clout of a half-dozen oil-producing developing nations. Whatever their other differences, there is agreement among most of the students of the problem that any effective reply to OPEC's power must be based on a wide number of American and Western stratagems.

The OPEC members are sensitive to the potential power of the industrialized world to dominate them, aware that time is running against them as their oil reserves are depleted, and wary of forcing intolerable burdens on Western economies, from which they ultimately derive their own economic strength. They know—and most Washington strategists agree—that a military response to their monopoly power would be highly dubious from the West's viewpoint. But they, like Washington, cannot completely rule it out if the consequences of their oil prices become severe enough.

How to meet OPEC's threat to the Western economies, however, quickly divides the strategists into two schools. One group believes that world oil is an exhaustible resource that is running out in the foreseeable future. The other believes that oil supplies are still plentiful but are made scarce by OPEC's monopolistic control. Believers in the first school suggest that there is no effective short-term counter to OPEC and that there is a silver lining in the current crisis because it forces conservation and a turn toward alternative sources of energy. The second school argues that a competitive oil market, if the United States can produce a strategy to create it, could lower prices, increase production, and eventually destroy the monopoly.

It is typical of U.S. energy policy over the past decade that President Carter has wavered between both schools. Last February he said that it was an "idle hope" to try to destroy OPEC. But by June he was arguing that the world could not acquiesce to OPEC's dictates.

But, according to experts, many of the dramatic and popular proposals to oppose those dictates—such as using the food weapon, blocking Arab investments in the United States, and forming a consumers' cartel—simply will not work. Although the United States dominates world food markets the way OPEC controls oil, most OPEC nations have small populations, so their demand for food does not begin to match the West's demand for energy. Moreover, OPEC could always turn to Argentina or Australia for grain. Clamping down on the $35 billion worth of Arab-owned assets in the United States and preventing additional investments would deliver a far greater blow to world financial markets than to OPEC, which must find ways to "recycle" $70 billion worth of surplus oil revenues before June 1980. And though France has long advocated a consumers' cartel to hold a "dialogue" with OPEC, Washington has refused such an international conference because—at this point, at least—the West lacks the unity of economic interest that binds OPEC.

This does not mean that there is nothing the United States can do to counteract OPEC. Carter's proposal for U.S. oil import quotas is one way to halt the growing tide of U.S. imports and reduce pressure on world oil prices. But his critics argue that it will inevitably lead to allocation of imported oil, the same kind of government-administered system that is generally conceded to have worsened the present shortage.

Some students of the problem propose reviving the market apparatus. The most prominent proposal is by Professor Morris A. Adelman of the Massachusetts Institute of Technology, who has long argued for auctioning rights to U.S. oil imports. Adelman believes that the current world shortage is largely the result of the cartel and that the way to break its grip is to make it easy for OPEC members to cheat on each other.

"We could put up import entitlements for a monthly auction by sealed bid," he suggested. "Some 200 million tickets worth $2.5 billion would be up for grabs each month. Tickets could be bought anonymously through front men. A cartel country would sell oil at the current price, and not even customers would know the seller was rebating to the United States Treasury by buying tickets. Any country needing extra revenue would secretly buy more tickets to sell more barrels."

Opponents argue that Adelman's scheme will not work because spare production capacity lies almost completely with Saudi Arabia, and to some extent with Kuwait, and that both countries can afford to produce less to keep the cartel functioning. But Adelman argues that secret oil sales made to the United States by some Arab producers during the 1973–1974 embargo proves his system can work if the purchases are kept secret.

Another proposal studied since 1974 is to reduce imports by making foreign oil more expensive with the imposition of an ad valorem tax. But to be fully effective, such a plan requires that the price of domestic oil be allowed to hit world oil prices immediately, an inflationary option. Also, the United States would have to reach agreement with other oil consumers to fix equivalent taxes.

One obvious but difficult strategy involves breaking OPEC's grip by encouraging non-OPEC producers to put more of their oil on the world market. John Connally and Governor Jerry Brown have proposed a "North American energy Common Market" to deal with the many economic issues—including oil —that affect the relations among the United States, Mexico, and Canada.

In Mexico's case, the United States might agree to import more Mexican foodstuffs and ease immigration restraints in return for increased production from Mexico's burgeoning oil and gas reserves. Some of that oil could be slipping through Washington's fingers. Japan is negotiating to buy 6 percent of Mexican production in return for Japanese plant equipment, adding to world supply but dragging it to market halfway around the globe.

Canada is still a net importer of energy, and its National Energy Board would permit large-scale exports only after a major and highly political settlement of a number of issues between the two countries, including renegotiation of the pact that governs duty-free exchange of auto products.

Along the same lines, the United States has begun to push international lending agencies into energy. The World Bank estimates that by the 1980s, 11 percent of its lending will be for energy projects. This is not likely to develop new large oil exports, but by increasing the world oil pool it could reduce the leverage of the major exporters.

There are those who also suggest that Washington has an option to intervene with military force in the Middle East should OPEC's actions become too threatening. In a new study for Congress, John M. Collins and Clyde R. Mark, of the Congressional Research Service, conclude that five American divisions could be mustered, with difficulty, and defeat the OPEC armed forces in the Persian Gulf. "But that could produce a Pyhrric victory if our prize were ruined in the process," their study says. "Presuming sufficient installations remained intact to serve U.S. and/or allied petroleum interest, constant security against skullduggery would still remain a challenge." Guarding against that, the report concludes, would weaken the U.S. defenses elsewhere around the globe.

A powerful group of experts in the U.S. intelligence community and in the State Department, however, do not believe in a confrontation with OPEC at all. Most OPEC producers, they argue, have "valid conservationist" reasons for keeping production at current levels. And the higher price for oil encourages the United States to move faster on programs for conservation and new energy development.

Although their counsel is little heard in the media, they have had an enormous influence on government decision-making. They believe that the way to weaken OPEC's sting is to work closely with the oil-producing nations on a bilateral basis. That was, in part, the origin of the so-called special relationship with

Saudi Arabia. Though that has lately waned, some link the recent sale of American weapons to the Saudis with their decision to lift oil production by 12 percent.

But it seems clear that until a more effective domestic energy program is put into place, the leverage that the United States has on OPEC is likely to be minimal. And that will reinforce the voices of those inside and outside government who argue that cooperation rather than confrontation with OPEC should be the U.S. policy.

After two oil crises and two recessions—and years after OPEC captured control over the world's oil supply—the U.S. Government has yet to come up with any comprehensive energy policy that could deal with the forthcoming problems of the 1980s. The Carter administration's grand plan for energy did not provide a set of definitive guidelines and solutions for the country but instead triggered off a massive controversy in Congress and around the nation that may in the end leave the United States just as vulnerable to energy crises in the 1980s as it was in the 1970s. Despite some very important progress in conserving energy and curbing waste, Washington has not achieved the crucial goal of helping to ensure reliable supplies of energy at reasonable prices.

The latest effort in Washington's attempt to alter the shape of the country's energy policy is the Carter administration's big push into synthetic fuels. As originally proposed in the summer of 1979, while the memory of long gas lines lingered in the minds of most Americans, the plan called for:

• $88 billion to be spent on dozens of huge synfuel plants around the country;

• $16.5 billion for mass transportation improvements;

• $24 billion to help the poor pay for higher-priced energy, especially home heating oil;

• $13.7 billion for a series of grants, subsidies, and tax credits allocated for the development of solar power and dozens of other projects designed to cut back on oil imports;

• Quotas on oil imports that would limit them to the peak level reached in 1977—8.5 million barrels a day.

The total package came to a neat $142.2 billion, and the idea at the time was to finance it entirely from a windfall profits tax on the oil companies, which would receive a lot more for their oil because of the decontrol on domestic crude-oil prices already passed by Carter.

But from the moment President Carter opened his mouth, Congress was ready to tear apart his energy plan—and it proceeded to do so at a rapid pace throughout the fall and winter of 1979. The Senate Finance Committee, under the direction of its chairman, Senator Russell B. Long of Louisiana, passed a huge list of exemptions from Carter's windfall profits tax. The tax was eliminated on newly discovered oil, and the committee was under pressure to do the same on stripper, tertiary, and Alaskan oil. Tax credits were passed to encourage conservation by businesses and homeowners. That was fine, but in the end the Senate committee passed enough exemptions from the windfall profits tax to eliminate virtually all of the proposed $142.2 billion income it was supposed to produce. And without that cash, the synfuel industry would not get its $88 billion to start up a new energy industry.

In fact, even before Congress started paring back the windfall profits tax, it had already cut back the huge synfuels plan to the point where it proposed financing only ten pilot plants for $20 billion—and even that was up in the air. If Congress left the windfall profits tax kitty empty, that $20 billion would have to come from general tax appropriations, and that would increase the federal budget deficit, which was already bloated.

Congress went its own way on energy and opted to move away from a heavily government-supported synfuel program, to rely instead on greater drilling within the United States to increase domestic production. By increasing exemptions to the windfall profits tax on decontrolled crude oil, Congress hoped that the tens of billions of additional dollars flowing into the pockets of the major U.S. oil companies would produce a lot more domestic crude for the country. Unfortunately, Congress did not bother to check out the recent history of drilling in the United States. If it had, it would have seen that drilling was no longer doing what it had done historically—raise U.S. oil production. Higher profits for the oil companies may lead to greater drilling, but that probably will not result in more domestic crude or American energy independence.

At the same time, the evisceration of Carter's energy program proved once again that leadership is crucial in solving the problem of America's decline in power. Energy dependence will remain one of the major causes of continued U.S. economic weakness in the decade ahead unless something dramatic is done.

The congressional action also showed that in Washington there is as yet no consensus on fundamental energy issues. Washington policy-makers are split on what roles government and private industry should play in solving the energy crisis. They are split on whether free markets should play the leading part in reducing the country's dependence or whether the government should have the biggest role. Furthermore, they are split over how much emphasis to put on conservation and how much on raising production.

To be sure, some progress has been made in Washington to help solve the urgent energy problem. Congress and Presidents, from Nixon to Ford to Carter, have already agreed to a number of measures that may save up to 3 or 4 million barrels a day by 1985. They have muscled Detroit into producing far more fuel-efficient automobiles while knocking down the speed limit to 55 miles per hour. They have decided to raise prices on domestically produced crude oil and gas to world levels by decontrolling them. They are providing tax incentives to homeowners and industry to promote conservation of energy and to encourage them to switch from oil to gas and coal. And finally, government energy research has been broadened to include solar power and other exotic sources of energy instead of focusing only on nuclear power.

Moreover, the market itself, through the sharp run-up in price, has forced a trimming of energy demands. The United States is slowly changing its gluttonous habits; overall growth in demand for oil and electricity has been cut in half since 1973.

But this has hardly been enough to prevent the gas lines from reappearing in the summer of 1979. Washington action has been agonizingly slow. President Nixon first asked Congress for gas deregulation and decontrol in 1974. Congress didn't act until 1979, and the price ceiling finally will not come off gas until 1985. The same irritating snail's pace is also responsible for congressional resistance to freeing domestic crude-oil prices, which will not reach world levels until 1981. And of course, there remain controls on gasoline prices, which are one-half to one-third the price in Europe or Japan. "We've gone 10 miles when we should have gone 80," complained House Interior Committee Chairman Morris K. Udall of Arizona.

The changing structure of Congress has been partly to blame for its slowness in acting on energy. Reacting against the Nixon era and the Vietnam War, Congress has passed reforms that weaken the power of the committee chairmen and decentralize responsibility. Congressional leadership has declined sharply since the Johnson years, and Congress has found it increasingly difficult to act on anything in recent years.

Beyond that, very deep regional differences have hampered congressional action on energy. "The Senate is almost evenly divided between oil-producing states and oil-consuming states," said one top Senate aide. It took a deal that gave something to states that do not produce gas to end a decades-old fight in the Senate over natural-gas pricing. Deregulation meant higher prices and costs for the non-gas-producing states.

In the White House, President Nixon was mired in the Watergate scandal when the first energy crisis hit, in 1973. It paralyzed his ability to act when OPEC launched its embargo, and the United States remained silent when, a few months later, OPEC raised the oil price fourfold. Gerald Ford could have had a tremendous impact back in 1975 when he was faced with legislation that reimposed controls on new oil production. He could have vetoed the Energy Policy and Conservation Act of 1975 but decided in the end not to antagonize Congress.

It is to his credit that President Carter from the start of his administration saw energy as a crucial policy area. When he took office in 1977, Carter's first priority was to send Congress a comprehensive energy program that included a wellhead tax on oil that would have sent domestic prices charged refiners up to world levels by 1980, continued regulation of natural gas but at a higher price, and a package of tax credits and mandatory measures that aimed at greater conservation and a larger use of coal.

But Carter's lack of leadership and lack of understanding of Congress gutted his early attempt at an energy program. His people lost control of the program in the Senate. Instead of sending up a broadly defined package that left room for the normal wrangling and compromising that occurs in Congress, they put together a very detailed program that already reflected many compromises made within the administration. For example, the plan called for a price of $1.75 per 1000 cubic feet of natural gas. That price was the highest figure acceptable to officials who wanted to control gas and the lowest price acceptable to officials favoring deregulation. "When it got up here, it had gone through so many political compromises already that there weren't any left for us to make," complained a top aide to one key Senate chairman. "We have to be able to make political compromises to legislate effectively."

Moreover, lack of leadership within the Carter administration hurt energy legislation. The early freewheeling days when anyone spoke his mind without conforming to the administration's line confused Congress. "Instead of having one voice, they have three voices on energy—the White House, the Office of Management and Budget, and the Energy Department," pointed out House Energy Subcommittee Chairman John D. Dingell at the time.

The effectiveness of the Carter administration's second attempt, in 1979, to pass energy programs will surely be tested in the 1980s. In the few short months between the summer and fall of 1979, Congress decided to overhaul completely the original package; it remains to be seen whether Congress's ideas on energy can break U.S. dependence on foreign oil. But one thing is clear, and Udall expressed it perfectly: "Energy is going to dominate our politics for a long time. It's going to dominate our lives."

Seven Sisters

Of course, it was not long ago that the United States—or at least its major oil companies—dominated energy. The connection between oil and power long predates the creation of OPEC, and if anything, the history of the postwar world is one of a changing relationship between the giant American and British oil companies and the producers of oil.

If anything, the British seemed to recognize the connection between oil and power well before the United States. In 1905, for example, when oil was still used mainly for household illumination, His Majesty's Government dispatched troops from the Indian army to protect a British drilling crew that was searching for oil in Persia. After that crew made the first major oil strike in the Middle East, the British government made the imperial tie even closer by acquiring 51 percent of the company, now known as British Petroleum, that owned the fabulously rich Persian oil concession. Its £2 million investment has, of course, been returned more than a thousandfold.

It was the U.S. political standing with its own allies that gave Americans their first entry in the Mideast oil play. After World

War I, Britain and France claimed rights for their national oil companies to prewar concessions in Iraq, which had been part of the Ottoman Empire. The United States protested that this flew in the face of its open door policy, which mandated free trade for all with allied interests. Eventually, the French and British capitulated, and two U.S. companies—the Standard Oil Company of New York and Standard Oil of New Jersey—were cut in on the deal. (Standard Oil Company of New Jersey later changed its name to Exxon. Standard Oil of New York became, in 1931, Socony-Vacuum; in 1966 it became Mobil.)

Ironically, through the 1920s and into the 1930s, the growing American presence in the Mideast oil fields was looked on almost as a blessing by many Arab leaders. The United States, in effect, played a role similar to that of a white knight in a merger; in some Arab eyes, it kept the British Empire at bay. For example, in 1930 King Ibn-Saud was more than pleased to give sizable oil concessions to Texaco and Standard Oil of California (Socal), the original partners in Arabian-American Oil Company (Aramco), because he felt that Americans would balance the strong British influence in the area.

Because the Mideast countries were so rich in oil, it was not long before numerous Western oil companies got into the act. And in 1947 the disparate efforts of the companies started to coalesce. Exxon and Mobil were cut in by the two original Aramco partners, Exxon for a 30 percent slice of Aramco, and Mobil for 10 percent. Meanwhile, Gulf and British Petroleum, which had access to the rich oil strike in Kuwait, agreed to supply oil from that country to Shell and split the profits down the middle. The result was an informal prorating system for Mideast crude that soon led to the loose confederation that came to be known as the Seven Sisters.

Whether the Seven Sisters were ever a cartel in the true sense of the word is still a debated point. The U.S. Department of Justice certainly seemed to think so, to the point of attacking the arrangement, in 1952, in an antitrust suit. But British economist Paul H. Frankel insisted sometime afterward that the pro-rating system "made it simply unnecessary to have a cartel." The deals, he said, "obviated, or at least limited, the need for the comparative newcomers to fight their way into the international market and consolidated the position of those who took their crude."

What made the system work was the highly concentrated and integrated structure of the international oil industry. Through an intricate web of affiliates, the Seven Sisters operated most of the refineries and controlled most of the marketing outlets for their 85 percent chunk of overseas oil output. There was very little arm's-length trading in crude, and that was generally tied to long-term contracts. The lack of a free market in crude discouraged the building of refineries by anyone who was not associated at least indirectly with one of the majors. The informal policing inherent in joint concession also encouraged the majors to limit their crude "offtake" to what they could readily market themselves. With a cost of production of less than twenty-five cents a barrel, the Mideast concessions were veritable money machines, a fact that was hardly lost on the governments of producing countries.

The first blow to the Western-controlled system was Iran's attempt in 1951 to nationalize its oil fields, which had been under concession to British Petroleum since they were first discovered. Almost immediately, the British government, which still had its 51 percent interest in BP, sent warships to the Persian Gulf and evacuated British nationals, including all of the oil-field workers. Iran attempted to run the fields with the help of Russian technicians (a fact that accounted for some of the hostility of the U.S. Government toward the regime of Mohammed Mossadegh), but it never got production up beyond a minor fraction of its prenationalization level. And it even had trouble selling this much oil, since the majors, with the support of their respective governments, instituted a boycott of Iranian oil that was generally effective. "The lesson," international oil consultant Walter J. Levy observed later, "was that you can nationalize the oil but you can't nationalize the market." But, as was demonstrated twenty-eight years later, when another Iranian revolution shut down the fields, it was a lesson that worked only because there was enough spare capacity in the United States and elsewhere to fill the hole.

The return of the shah to power in 1953, with the help of the CIA, brought a settlement of the nationalization dispute that had its own particular problems. The American majors, of course, were cut in on the action, but at the insistence of the U.S. Justice Department, a number of independents also were given small stakes, which launched them into the international oil business for the first time. Not only did this weaken the majors' bargaining power with the governments of producer-states; it brought competition for the first time to a market that had been based on mutual forbearance. And this, in turn, made it more difficult for the majors to play their traditional role of maintaining prices in the face of a worldwide oil glut, a condition that was almost automatic when Iran suddenly came back on stream as the world's largest oil exporter. According to a veteran oil man, "The re-entry of Iran was the major factor that broke the international oil price at the end of the fifties and led to the establishment of OPEC."

The Rise of OPEC

Like its 1917 Russian namesake, OPEC's October revolution in 1973 overthrew a regime that was already in the process of coming apart. For decades, the Seven Sisters had shared their virtual monopoly on international oil traffic, but the entry of new and unexpected forces simply eroded their power. OPEC, therefore, was a cartel forged by producer-governments because the loose cartel of the companies was no longer working.

The power switch-over was gradual, of course. Concessions in the Middle East originally had provided for a flat royalty on each barrel produced. In 1948, however, Aramco negotiated a contract with King Ibn-Saud to split profits fifty-fifty, and that quickly set the pattern for the Middle East. As long as prices— and profits—were stable, the "equal partners" concept worked fine. It amounted to a tax of seventy-eight cents a barrel, which the companies could use to offset their taxes at home. With growing exports, it yielded a revenue rise of about 20 percent a year for most of the producer-governments. When the price began to fall and skim off some of the profits, though, it became a different story.

Initially, the price-shading took the form of discounts from posted prices, and the companies absorbed the losses. When prices refused to firm and profits began to decline, however, the companies responded with general reductions in posted prices, which automatically reduced the government's take. The first reduction, in February 1959, made the governments hopping mad; the second, in August 1960, got them to react much as workers would if their employer suddenly announced a cut in hourly wages because his products weren't selling too well: they organized.

The Organization of Petroleum Exporting Countries thus began in September 1960 as a sort of producers' union, and for the next decade its sole achievement was to keep posted prices from falling in line with market prices, which dropped steadily from $1.80 a barrel in 1960 to $1.45 in 1969. There was always some radical urging nationalization but the general attitude of OPEC members was that, as Sheikh Yamani put it in 1969, "the majors are the only means of market stability available at the present time." He warned, however, that "if they lose their power, they will lose their attraction for us."

What Yamani had in mind was the classic collision of majors and independents over Libyan oil. Libya was the first big oil strike since Kuwait in 1948, and the first to be developed primarily by independents. Previously, big oil had been found where one group had a whole country locked up. Libya, with an eye to speeding development, parceled out concessions to some fifteen or twenty groups—and added a tough relinquishment clause so that territory not immediately explored reverted to the government. Six of the seven majors got in on the first round, but so did a number of independents whose previous experience overseas had been in getting the U.S. Government to assign them a share of the Iranian consortium. The first Libyan strike was made by Exxon in 1958. The next year, the Oasis Oil Company made its joint owners—Continental Oil, Marathon, and Amerada-Hess—the first nonmajors with substantial overseas reserves. After that, oil strikes in Libya became an annual occurrence—and many of the big ones were by independents, including one inexperienced, undercapitalized company named Occidental Petroleum, which was subsequently to play a special role in the international oil business.

The pace of development in Libya was unprecedented. Oil began flowing in 1961, and within four years Libya was producing at a rate of 1.2 million barrels a day, a level that had taken Kuwait more than a decade to reach. By 1968, Libya's production had passed that of Kuwait, which had twice as much reserve as Libya, and the following year it even edged past Saudi Arabia's. Because of oil import controls, imposed as a voluntary program in 1957 and made mandatory in 1959, little of the oil could be sold in the United States. Thus, the only options that independents had was to come to terms with the majors or battle them for European markets. Enough chose the latter alternative for the effect on prices to be disastrous.

The U.S. oil import–control program had been intended right from the start to insulate the domestic industry, which had already formed a powerful lobby in Washington, from the effects of the international oil glut. By the late 1950s, the European market had been fairly well saturated, and Japan was also pretty well taken care of. The next logical move for Arab oil was to the U.S. East Coast, a prospect that appalled the purely domestic producers, who were themselves groaning under surplus capacity. A rigid quota system provided a breakwater against the expected wave of foreign crude. Imports were restricted to a set proportion of domestic demand—12.2 percent for the area east of the Rockies, for example. The short-term effect was to maintain a U.S. price that was higher than the international price by about $1.25 a barrel. The long-term effect, of course, was to encourage more U.S. production and deplete U.S. resources faster. Undertaken, in theory, on the grounds that U.S. national security required a vigorous American producing industry, the quota system was really, as John Lichtblau of the Petroleum Industry Research Foundation said years later, a "drain America first policy."

From Glut- to Scarcity-Mentality

The Libyans, apparently, had no intention of draining their reserves without reaping maximum profit. The Libyan revolution of September 1, 1969, brought to power a group of radicals who were willing to take some risks—including the risk of offending powerful companies and their home countries—to get more money for a product that was essential, depletable, and thus priced too low. Their reasoning was technical and eminently practical, not ideological. The closing of the Suez Canal in 1967 meant that oil originating in the Mediterranean suddenly had a definite cost advantage over oil produced in the Persian Gulf—oil that to this point still determined the going price of crude. What is more, stricter pollution controls in Europe meant enhanced value for the lower-sulfur oil that Libya produced.

Most petroleum economists agreed that the thirty cents per barrel increase the Libyans asked for in 1970 was more than justified by these two factors. But the American oil companies were far more concerned with maintaining the huge profit differential between the price they were getting for crude, which they were splitting with the Libyans, and the price of the finished refined product, which they kept for themselves. The chances are that if the majors felt that the price increase could have been confined to Libya, they would have reluctantly agreed to the price hike. But their main fear was that the Persian Gulf countries would quickly follow the Libyan example and that an unstoppable spiral of increased prices would begin.

The Libyans, of course, recognized that their insistence on price hikes would meet massive resistance from the majors as a group. What became important from the standpoint of the U.S. companies, then, was not whether the Libyans were justified, but how they would go about enforcing their demands. And their method was unerring in its simplicity: they looked for the weakest link in the Western oil chain. And they found it— Occidental Petroleum, which was the most dependent of the Western companies on Libyan oil. When Oxy balked at meeting Libya's price demands, the Qaddafi government ordered the company to cut back production.

It was a lethal pressure tactic, since Libya was the only source of crude that Oxy could draw on to fulfill commitments to its European customers. Oxy's resourceful chairman, Armand Hammer, made a valiant effort at fighting back—and, in fact, if the more powerful majors had rallied behind him, the crisis might have been averted. He first went to Exxon, for example, to make up the difference. Oil analysts are still trying to figure out why Exxon Chairman Edward Jamieson refused to supply the needed oil at a price that would have bailed out Oxy. But the fact is that he did refuse, and Hammer had to give in to Libyan demands.

As the majors had feared, the nightmarish upward spiral of crude prices started soon afterward. The other companies operating in Libya, including Exxon, shortly followed Hammer's agreement to raise prices. And, as expected, the Persian Gulf producers followed the Libyan example and asked the companies operating in their areas for more money.

In actuality, 1970 marked the first oil crisis, and in hindsight, it is apparent that it was the beginning of a turn from the glut-mentality to a growing shortage-panic. Although the rising prices seemed to be based on the political interests of the producing countries, they were also reflecting a change in the demand-supply relationship. The United States was, in truth, peaking in its production in the early 1970s, and the beginning of the switch of oil power from the West to the East was already in process.

The move was completed when Libya, seeking to restore the differential it had earlier established, made new price demands that the chastened oil companies were in no position to refuse. The process had become a game of leapfrog, and as the situation began to look dangerously unstable, the oil companies looked around for something to bring it under control.

What came to mind most immediately was OPEC, an organization that at the time had been considered almost irrelevant to the major events in the oil industry. After the U.S. companies had received clearance from the Justice Department for collective action, all of the international oil companies got together and issued a formal proposal to OPEC for a general settlement on prices that would include all oil companies and all producing countries. At the insistence of the producers, the negotiations were split into two sessions: one, for the Persian Gulf producers, was scheduled for Tehran in January 1971; the other, for all of the North African producers, was to be held subsequently in Tripoli.

By this time, it had become clear that the bargaining power of the oil producers vis-à-vis the oil companies had changed considerably from the days when there was a glut. The peaking of U.S. production was seen by the increasingly sophisticated technicians in OPEC as an indication that a new market was

World oil's paradox:
Bountiful reserves, slower production growth

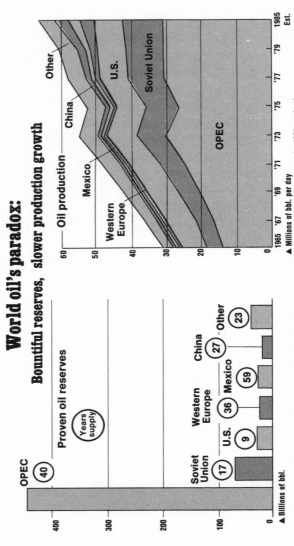

Proven oil reserves

(Years supply)

- OPEC **40**
- Soviet Union **17**
- U.S. **9**
- Western Europe **36**
- Mexico **59**
- China **27**
- Other **23**

▲ Billions of bbl.

Oil production

- Other
- China
- Mexico
- Western Europe
- U.S.
- Soviet Union
- OPEC

▲ Millions of bbl. per day

1965 '67 '69 '71 '73 '75 '77 '79 1985 Est.

Note: Reserves are for yearend 1978. Oil supply in years is determined by dividing reserves by 1978 production.
Data: *Oil & Gas Journal*, Pemex, DeGolyer & MacNaughton, Platt's *Oligram News*, BW estimate.

Courtesy of Business Week

about to open up, one that would take all of the oil they would want to produce. The companies eventually agreed to a 15 percent increase in the posted price, with a provision for a 2.5 percent annual price rise for the following five years. The oil companies thought of that as a pretty expensive settlement but welcomed the idea of a long period of stability, which was what oil men valued above almost everything else. The stability, of course, lasted less than three years.

The catalyst for the final stage of OPEC's rise to power was the Yom Kippur War, which began on October 5, 1973. The war was accompanied by a selective boycott by Arab oil producers that was aimed principally at the United States, which after the war undertook a massive effort to resupply Israel with military equipment lost in the initial battles. It was not the first time the oil weapon had been unsheathed, but it was the first time the United States could be hurt. The Arab oil producers had attempted a boycott during the Six Day War of 1967, but it was ineffective because the United States simply increased its own oil production, which was then running at only 75 percent of capacity, to make up for lessened Arab production. Five years later, however, the United States had no surplus capacity. Though it was not itself particularly dependent on Arab oil, the 10 percent cutback in Arab production created a worldwide shortage of crude that made the European countries and Japan eager to secure a special place on the supply schedule. To curry favor with the Arabs, Europeans even denied landing and re-fueling rights to American planes engaged in resupplying Israel. It was the first time in recent history that an economic threat had direct military implications. As one oil analyst summarized the situation: "What really helped OPEC was the picture of the most powerful countries in the world scrambling after a product that was owned by a group of rich but under-developed—and presumably powerless—Third World nations. It was a revolution in every sense of the word."

Clearly, OPEC was beginning to feel its power. And although

the West at this point could still handle the supply cutoff without massive dislocations, the seemingly endless price increases had a drastically deleterious impact. Coincidental with the cutoff of Arab oil was a previously scheduled meeting by the OPEC countries at which, for the first time, the organization set prices without even talking to the oil companies. But the boost to $5.00 a barrel left the posted price of oil well below the $15 or more that oil was fetching on the spot market. The Shah of Iran, who had not been part of the oil boycott and had actually allowed increases in oil production at a time when the Arabs were cutting back, was the most adamant about the need for a truly massive increase in the price of oil. Shortly before the price hike, the shah warned in an interview with an Italian journalist that an increase in price "is a solution brought on by your overcivilized industrial society. You've increased the price of wheat by three hundred percent, and the same for sugar and cement. You've sent the price of petrochemicals skyrocketing . . . You make us pay more for everything, scandalously more, and it's only fair that from now on you should pay more for oil. Let's say . . . ten times more."

The actual increase in 1974 was not quite that much—at least, not right away. The price was jacked up by "only" four times its preboycott level. And the West could do nothing about it but complain—and prepare to increase its payments to the oil cartel by a cool $100 billion a year. Never before in history had there been such an enormous transfer of wealth.

According to Zbigniew Brzezinski, President Carter's national security adviser, Third World leaders "have noted that the year 1973 will go down in history as equal in importance to the year 1905, which marked the first time a European power [Russia] was defeated by a non-European power [Japan] . . . [It] is seen as marking the first significant victory by the developing countries over the advanced countries in the economic realm."

The Embattled
Multinationals

Growth Amid the Ruins

No institution has been more closely identified with the growth of America's world role in this century than the United States–based multinational corporation. From the defeat of the Axis powers in 1945 through the mid 1970s, the astounding surge in U.S. corporate activity overseas has both benefited from and sustained America's image as the planet's pre-eminent power. Understandably, to many foreigners the multinationals are America.

In Singapore, São Paulo, Paris, Toronto, and dozens of other cities, the neon logos of U.S. corporations light the night skies of the world. Coca-Cola, blue jeans, IBM computers, and John Deere tractors shape consumer tastes and business policies around the world. No other single nation's business community owns as much as a quarter of the holdings of American corporations abroad. At well over $300 billion, the sales of U.S. foreign affiliates dwarf the gross national products of all but the largest nations in the world. So awesome has been the influence of the U.S. multinationals on the world economy that their critics attribute to them the power to dominate local governments, even to force national treasuries to devalue their currencies by betting against them in global money markets.

Yet after three decades of continued growth, the managers and strategists of American multinationals viewed the world of the late 1970s as fraught with danger. Their doubts about overseas prospects stemmed not only from the erosion of U.S.

power, but from an array of dangers that seemed to grow more fearsome because of it. Nationalistic economic policies among less developed countries were becoming more forceful and sophisticated. Competition from European and Japanese multinationals—backed, financed, and often wholly or partly owned by their home governments—became fierce. And unanimously, executives of U.S. multinationals regarded Washington's regulatory maze and indifference often bordering on outright hostility to their interests abroad as key factors in crimping their sales overseas and jeopardizing the security of their investments.

The multinational corporate community encounters Washington as an adversary in many of the things it is involved in overseas. Antibribery and antiboycott laws severely curb the activities of American multinationals abroad, but no other major industrial power puts such harsh restraints on its own corporations. Meanwhile, the government, executives charge, simply has no effective policy for backing American overseas business. "You learn from experience not to call for help from our government," said the head of one of the largest U.S. banks in Tokyo. "You just don't waste your time."

Understanding the sea-changes in the world of the U.S. multinationals requires a look back in time. International enterprise has been part of American life almost from the birth of the nation. (The American Revolution was sparked, in part, by protest against British tea taxes collected by one of the earliest multinationals, the British East India Company.) As early as the 1850s, some fifty large U.S. corporations were engaged in sizable ventures abroad. Later, as European nations staked out sprawling empires in Africa and Asia as exclusive trade and investment preserves for British, French, and German companies, America's Monroe Doctrine helped ensure that Latin America would remain open to U.S. investment. By the 1890s, American companies, such as the Guggenheim mining interests, were garnering fortunes from investment south of the Rio Grande.

American business interest in foreign trade and investment

took a quantum leap after the Spanish-American War. The existence of the new American empire, especially the Philippines colony, encouraged businessmen to envision the tapping of a vast "China market." By the outbreak of World War I, American companies' holdings abroad (principally in Canada, Europe, Mexico, and Asia), had grown to roughly 7 percent of the U.S. gross national product (GNP).

Still, foreign investment remained peripheral to the U.S. economy. Most corporations, including the giants spawned by the mergers of the late 1800s, concentrated mainly on meeting the demands of America's vast, integrated continental market. Between the two world wars, troubled international relations, trade wars, and the Great Depression kept most U.S. companies from deepening their stakes abroad. But as A. D. Chandler showed in his study, *Strategy and Structure,* the Depression also forced a major rethinking of their strategies by the leading U.S. corporations. Moving beyond the quest for dominance in single lines of business or markets, America's most dynamic companies sought to diversify both their products and markets.

The massive surge in business output during World War II (the U.S. GNP more than doubled between Pearl Harbor and 1945), and the managerial expertise gained by American enterprises, placed the leading U.S. corporations in a position to diversify their products and markets on a worldwide basis. Geared to meet wartime demands, corporations like Kaiser (shipbuilding, aluminum), Goodyear (rubber), Boeing (aerospace), and others had become accustomed to production on a scale hitherto unheard of, as well as the management and servicing of production across international boundaries.

In the wake of Japan's surrender, these corporations faced a rare opportunity. Britain was nearly bankrupt, its industries obsolescent. German and Japanese factories were bomb-blasted ruins. Much of Europe was insolvent, and, however militarily powerful, the Soviet Union was reeling from the bloodiest war in history. There simply were no competitors on earth for the

huge, undamaged behemoths that America's largest corporations had become during the war. And soon U.S. Government
policy was to aid their surge of expansion abroad.

With millions of workers unemployed, western Europe, the
heartland of capitalism, was haunted by fears of communist
revolution. In what would soon be called the Third World,
nationalist rebellions were unraveling the empires of Britain,
France, and Holland from Casablanca to Saigon. Market forces
alone appeared helpless to stimulate the world's revival. The
U.S. Government took the lead.

In an unprecedented aid operation, more than $10 billion in
Marshall Plan grants financed the reconstruction of the shat-
tered economies of both wartime Allies and defeated enemies.
In the process, the United States dispelled the specter of communism in western Europe and ensured the survival of democratic, free-enterprise governments. Throughout the ensuing
Cold War with the Soviet Union, the administrations of Presidents Truman, Eisenhower, and Kennedy were firmly behind
the security of governments friendly to free enterprise, and
U.S. investors. Under the Truman Doctrine, enunciated in 1947,
America pledged resistance to violent revolutions led by radical
nationalists or Soviet-aligned communist movements. Through
the climax of the Cold War during the 1962 Cuban missile crisis,
the United States was ready, as John F. Kennedy had put it in
his inaugural, "to go anywhere, bear any burden, pay any price"
in defense of America's vision of the free world.

Backing Washington's political commitment was a series of
alliances, centered on the North Atlantic Treaty Organization
(NATO), that called for the United States to aid its friends in
resisting invasion. Elsewhere, American policy unashamedly
opposed radical movements in the Third World that threatened
to displace foreign investments. American military bases
abroad mushroomed from a handful before World War II to
more than 2000 installations by the mid 1950s. More subtly, the

new Central Intelligence Agency was increasingly active. In the early 1950s, for example, the CIA moved to counter radical governments intent on seizing Western oil holdings in Iran (mainly those of British Petroleum) and on nationalizing the plantations of United Fruit (now part of United Brands) in Guatemala. The governments of both Iran and Guatemala were overthrown by groups enjoying CIA backing, and in Iran, Mohammed Reza Pahlavi, the Shah of Iran, came to power. Several U.S. oil companies were soon invited, as we have seen, to share BP's former monopoly of Iranian oil. In that era of sharp political and ideological conflict, in short, Washington was willing and able to engage in a modern version of gunboat diplomacy in defense of U.S. interests overseas.

Throughout the early postwar period and into the 1950s, that willingness to act helped form a relatively stable world, one that was amenable to the growth of U.S. multinationals. Other government policies, ranging from the expenditure of billions of dollars in foreign aid (most of it tied to purchases of U.S. goods), tax legislation, and government insurance for, and credit to, U.S. companies trading or investing abroad, spurred the expansion of American multinationals.

Washington's international economic policies—on currencies, trade, and investment—were also crucial. As agreed at the wartime Bretton Woods Conference, the American dollar steadily supplanted the British pound as the main denominator of world trade and the key reserve currency. Pegged to gold at $35 an ounce, the dollar served as a financial anchor against the kind of volatile currency fluctuations that had been seen between the world wars. Throughout the 1950s and 1960s, the dollar's continued strength against all major currencies enabled U.S. multinationals to finance expansion abroad more easily and cheaply than ever before.

U.S. trade policy, beginning with the first postwar round of the General Agreement on Tariffs and Trade (GATT), consistently boosted liberal policies toward trade and investment. In that, American policy succeeded beyond the imagination of its most fervent postwar supporters. From 1945 to 1975, world trade grew at a rate of more than 10 percent a year, far outstripping the growth of the world economy. Much of that trade was done by United States–based multinationals or their foreign subsidiaries. Thus, American governmental policy and multinational corporate strategies moved in tandem through one of the most rapid economic expansions in Western history.

During the 1950s and early 1960s serious conflicts between Washington and American multinationals were almost nonexistent. The outreach of U.S. corporations for global markets and facilities was regarded in America as beneficial both at home and abroad. World production was being integrated and rationalized in a way never before seen, and the multinationals seemed the vehicle for realizing every nation's "comparative advantage" by freely combining labor, raw materials, and capital to maximize efficiency. American business techniques, developed in the huge home market, revolutionized the practices of European competitors. In electronics, telecommunications, aerospace, and cybernetics, U.S. multinationals were at the cutting edge of technical progress. Government and business shared a consensus: support for the growth of free enterprise and economic output worldwide.

The authors of a recent study by the Conference Board, a business-supported research organization, sum up the importance of that consensus.

> U.S. political influence in creating a pattern of economic relations in which the multinationals flourished and expanded in the post-war period should not be underestimated. The expansion of U.S. multinationals abroad occurred, at least in part, because it was in the political interest of the world's dominant power for them to do so. An economic policy that encouraged the free flow of goods and capital among non-communist countries, and hence an interdependent international economy, served U.S. security interests while it stimu-

lated unprecedented growth among the industrial countries. These were fertile conditions for the growth of [U.S.] multinationals...

And grow they did. From less than $5 billion in 1945, the direct investments of U.S. companies abroad multiplied more than twentyfold, to over $150 billion in 1979. Even that figure sharply understates the impact of American multinationals on the global economy. A more accurate gauge may be their total output of goods and services, which is now estimated at about 10 percent of the total world product.

The corporations that have led the multinational investment drive are, by any measure, the largest, most powerful, and fastest-growing enterprises in America. And the immense movement of capital and technology overseas that they have guided has radically altered the links between America and the world, binding the United States and other nations in a growing interdependence. Harvard Business School professor Raymond Vernon's *Storm Over the Multinationals* conveys the multinationals' growing significance: "In the United States, large firms that could reasonably have been classified as multinationals in 1950 accounted for only 17% of total U.S. sales of manufacturers. By 1967, the U.S. firms that were then multinational accounted for 42% of U.S. sales and, by 1974, for 62%."

Among the 500 corporations cited by *Fortune* magazine in its annual survey of the largest U.S. industrial enterprises, more than two-thirds now derive 25 percent or more of their sales and profits from the operations of overseas subsidiaries and affiliates. For the corporations at the top of that scale, foreign operations are even more vital. Ford Motor Company, for example, drew 48 percent of its 1978 sales from overseas operations. Ford products are made in dozens of countries by subsidiaries, licensees, and affiliates. Many of these operations are major enterprises in their own right. Similarly, in 1978 International Business Machines drew 52 percent of its $21 billion in total sales from abroad. The largest U.S. banks, too, have trekked around the globe to serve their U.S. corporate clients and open new accounts with foreigners. Citibank, America's most rapidly growing bank, derived more than 80 percent of its 1978 profits from its operations in ninety-three foreign countries.

In terms of both sales and profits, U.S. multinationals have grown almost without interruption over the past three decades —at a rate faster than the domestic economy or that of the world as a whole. From 1960 to 1975, the average annual sales growth of the 100 leading U.S. multinationals was over 12 percent; during the same period, the U.S. GNP advanced less than 5 percent a year. Even during the global recession of 1974–1975, the worst business downturn since the Great Depression, the twenty-five largest U.S. multinationals chalked up sales gains. "Going multinational," with the attendant capacity to scan world markets, borrow working and investment capital wherever it is cheapest, combine labor and machinery in an optimally efficient "global assembly line," has proved not only the most profitable avenue of postwar business growth, but the best strategy for long-term survival. Companies confined to one national market are at severe disadvantages in competition with those that span several. Indeed, Steven Hymer, a political economist, estimated that by 1990 more than 60 percent of the free world's output will be produced by just 300 firms, about 150 of them American multinationals.

The sheer weight of the multinationals in the U.S. economy is highlighted by their contributions to America's balance of payments. In most years since 1958, the United States has run a chronic balance-of-payments deficit with the rest of the world (measured by the total flow of goods, services, fees, and capital). But throughout this period of their growth abroad, United States–based multinationals have actually been net importers of capital from the rest of the world. In 1977, for example, while U.S. companies drew an estimated $15 billion from their earnings or borrowings in the United States to invest abroad, they sent home more than $25 billion in the forms of repatriated profits, license and patent fees, and home office management charges. Without that sizable surplus flow of cash to America, the U.S. balance-of-payments deficit would have had an even more devastating impact on the value of the dollar than it has had.

Equally significant is the role the multinationals play in supporting U.S. exports. The thousands of foreign affiliates and subsidiaries of the U.S. multinational network provide a worldwide captive market for the export of U.S. machinery, components, and services. Nearly one third of America's $140 billion in total manufactured exports in 1978 was sold to the overseas branches of American companies.

Success Breeds Reaction

But the very size of this foreign investment has opened multinationals to a barrage of criticism abroad and, more recently, at home. To some degree, foreign reaction against U.S. multinationals was inevitable. Success breeds envy and fear, and no economic institution in history has ever grown so rapidly or posed such profound challenges to their competitors. Foreign governments, especially those in the emerging Third World of the 1960s, often saw themselves as pawns in the game-plans of firms whose sales dwarfed their gross national products. Even in Europe and Canada, leading politicians and economists warned of the dangers to national sovereignty posed by U.S. corporate influence in local economies.

Because of their inextricable link with U.S. power, American multinationals also became the targets of foreign protesters, terrorists, and kidnapers who opposed U.S. policy, most notably America's role in Vietnam. Ironically, as the 1970s rolled on, Washington's inability to work its will on the outside world also emboldened once-hesitant foreign competitors and nationalist-minded (though conservative) foreign governments who wished to act against U.S. multinationals. Those challenges—

political and ideological criticism, revolutionary violence, and stiffening foreign competition—now combine to create a dangerous world for American multinationals. The erosion of their security, and the blurring of their image as the bearers of progress and prosperity, have resulted in part from the series of geopolitical blows to U.S. power that began with and were intensified by the disastrous war in Vietnam.

Vietnam was no ordinary war; it was a national trauma that profoundly affected the world's view of America, distorted the domestic economy, and ultimately undermined the strength of U.S. multinationals. Throughout the war's most intense phase, from 1965 to 1970, Presidents Johnson and Nixon watched a quick counterinsurgency "mop-up" deteriorate into a bloody, grueling ordeal. The war divided and polarized Americans more seriously than any other event of the twentieth century, and it squandered much of the good will America had built up abroad since 1945. U.S. troops found themselves mired in indecisive combat with a tough, elusive enemy. But the sheer weight of American air- and seapower made the United States seem a violent bully to many foreigners. Demonstrations against the American intervention racked cities around the globe. America's allies largely refused to become involved in the U.S. war effort. In the end, the American pull-out in 1975 left the United States demoralized, wary of foreign involvement, and looking, as Richard Nixon put it, like "a pitiful, helpless giant."

For American multinationals, the economic consequences of the war were worse than the military and political debacle. U.S. multinationals held only tiny stakes in South Vietnam before its fall. Despite the investment by the U.S. Government of billions of dollars to develop South Vietnam's infrastructure—roads, ports, and communications—American multinationals had trivial direct investments in the country, amounting to less than $50 million, by 1975. The few U.S. subsidiaries still in business when the North Vietnamese army overran Saigon (such as Philco-Ford's $32 million-plus transport and motor repair program) were minor extensions of their vast corporate parents. They were also insured against loss by the U.S. Government. But if the immediate stakes in South Vietnam were slight for the multinationals, the war's impact at home was deadly serious.

Politically unwilling to tax the people for an unpopular war, President Lyndon Johnson financed the U.S. effort in Vietnam (and the Great Society social welfare programs at home) by deficit spending. As the war's cost ratcheted over $35 billion a year by 1968, Johnson's policies for paying for it, and the similar course adopted by Richard Nixon, helped entrench inflationary expectations into the American economy. As the vast spending overseas to support the Vietnam effort piled up so many off-shore dollars, the U.S. currency came under increasing speculative pressure as the war dragged on. By August 1971, with foreign pressure mounting and domestic inflation close to 10 percent, President Nixon was forced to suspend the convertibility of the dollar into gold—thus destroying the foundation of the post–World War II monetary order. Nixon also imposed wage and price controls on the U.S. economy and decreed a special 10 percent tariff on imports to the United States. That unilateral gesture shocked American trading partners, particularly Japan. The war in Vietnam, in short, had by 1971 knocked loose two of the pillars of the world system that had provided strength for the U.S. multinational corporations: the stable dollar and the U.S. Government's steady commitment to free trade.

From 1971 on, U.S. multinationals were forced to adapt to a world in which currencies could fluctuate sharply within days and in which the American dollar was more or less steadily in decline. Investment abroad had become more precarious, too, partly because Washington had been unable to win the war. As one top official of a major U.S. bank put it: "It was easy in the pre-Vietnam days to look at an area on the map and say, 'That's ours,' and feel pretty good about investing there. That is no longer the case . . ."

The Vietnam War's political consequences at home were also

thoroughly disturbing to the multinationals. The antiwar protest that swept across American society eroded the authority of
all institutions and unleashed attacks on the multinationals
themselves—beginning with demonstrations against companies like Dow Chemical Company because of its manufacture
of the napalm used in Vietnam. In the late 1960s and early
seventies, American labor unions began to charge the multinationals with exporting U.S. jobs to cheap labor pools abroad.
Academics tagged them as the vehicles of a new American
imperialism. Legislation to curb their export of capital and to
tax their foreign operations more heavily was proposed (notably
in the Burke-Hartke bill), and nearly passed. For the first time,
American multinationals found themselves pilloried at home as
the cause of the slow growth, high unemployment, and corro-
sive inflation of the 1970s in the United States.

    Worse still, in the wake of the Watergate scandals, the out-
lines of what was to be a long-running feud between the multinationals and the federal government began to emerge. Large
corporations were found to have contributed enormous sums
(often under considerable pressure) to the re-election campaign
of Richard Nixon in 1972. Like the opening of Pandora's box, the
Watergate investigations let loose a host of scandals concerning
the multinationals. Revelations of large-scale corporate bribery
by the Lockheed Corporation and other firms eventually
showed that dozens of America's largest corporations had dis-
pensed hundreds of millions of dollars in bribes to secure overseas sales. The governments of Japan and Italy were rocked by
revelations that some of their leading politicians had been
recipients of the corporate largess. In Holland, the exposé of the
relations between Lockheed and Prince Bernhard nearly top-
pled the House of Orange. Finally, a Senate subcommittee
chaired by Frank Church of Idaho disclosed that the International Telephone and Telegraph Corporation had proposed to
the Central Intelligence Agency a scheme for "destabilizing"
and deposing the elected government of Chile's socialist presi-

dent, Salvador Allende. The main result of the mid 1970s' multinational scandals in America has been a series of laws and government regulations to tighten federal controls on multinationals. These regulations have put U.S. companies at sharp
disadvantages in relation to the aggressive competition they are
meeting from European and Japanese companies all over the
world.

Overseas, the scandals have provided fresh ammunition to
the multinationals' most bitter critics—the radical and socialist
theorists of the Third World and their allies in Europe and
Japan. Rejecting the theories of economic development put
forward by orthodox economists like Walt Rostow in his *Stages
of Economic Growth,* Third World critics have evolved an influential and politically damaging analysis of the multinational
firm. Their arguments form a set of interlocking propositions:
(1) huge, sophisticated multinationals enjoy enormous bargaining leverage versus small, weak nation-states, whose sovereignty is thus "at bay"; (2) even if multinational investment
brings about overall growth in a less developed country (LDC),
the resulting wealth is concentrated in urban centers, in the
hands of foreign management and its local employees; (3) the
entrance of multinationals into any LDC diverts local financial
resources, thus drying up funds domestic businesses might have
used for their own growth; (4) any multinational's claims to
transfer technology and know-how are misleading because
most investment in LDCs consists of mere segments of a worldwide manufacturing operation that only the multinational can
assemble into finished products and market.

Though spokesmen for the multinationals have tried to
counter every element of this analysis, it has become an accepted thesis in world politics, cropping up repeatedly at
United Nations conferences and in trade talks between the
LDCs and the Western industrial nations. Nor are such antimul-
tinational arguments limited to nations ruled by radical
regimes. The socialist government of Allende's Chile did, in

fact, cite such arguments for its expropriation of the copper mines of Anaconda and Kennecott, adding that there would be no compensation because the companies were in arrears of huge sums of unpaid taxes. But seven years after the military coup that replaced Allende with a right-wing, probusiness military junta, the country's key copper mines still remain in the hands of the state-owned corporation, Codelco. Anaconda and Kennecott did receive some cash in compensation from the new regime, but that barely covered a half-decade of their annual profits before Allende took them over.

Similar nationalistic feeling has marked the decade-long takeover of American oil companies' foreign holdings by host governments. That process, begun by the revolutionary government of Mexico in 1938, has been carried forward by the radical colonels in Libya, the moderate social democrats in Venezuela, and the deeply conservative monarchs in Saudi Arabia. Thus, the Aramco consortium, jointly owned by four of the most powerful U.S. oil companies (Exxon, Mobil, Socal, and Texaco), was wholly taken over in the 1970s by the Saudis, who gradually bought 100 percent of the ownership. Aramco's proven reserves are estimated at many billion dollars' worth of oil. But the consortium partners must now be content to serve as contractors for the Saudis, who control the level of output and even divert Aramco's liftings at will for sale by their own national oil company, Petromin.

Whatever their politics, governments all over the Third World are increasingly wary of control of their natural resources by U.S. (and other foreign) oil or mining companies. The trend toward reining the freewheeling ways of the extractive multinationals seems established beyond reversal.

Those U.S. multinationals engaged mainly in manufacturing and the development of high-technology products faced a different set of problems abroad in the 1960s and seventies. Their foreign investments—powered by the strong dollar of those years—have caused a backlash of fear, even in highly developed nations.

Perhaps the single deepest and broadest penetration of American corporate influence in any nation has taken place just above our northern border. Beginning with a relatively small stake at the turn of the century, American corporations have since sunk more than $60 billion into direct investments in Canada. The benefits to that country have been manifold: high capital–intensive projects that Canada's limited capital markets could not have financed have been accomplished. But by the late 1970s, American companies controlled more than 50 percent of all Canadian manufacturing. In key sectors, such as oil development and marketing, the American corporate share is even higher. Ninety-eight percent of Canada's oil refineries and petrochemical plants are owned and managed by U.S. companies. Nearly 100 percent of Canadian automobile production is done by Ford, General Motors, and Chrysler. U.S. corporate influence, in fact, has been a major issue in Canadian politics, with nationalists charging that the country has become a "branch plant" economy controlled by boards of directors of multinationals, based in New York, Chicago, and Detroit, that are not accountable to the Canadians. Because of the near-total intertwining of Canada's economy with that of the United States, brought about by multinational investment, some economists doubt that the government in Ottawa can effectively control its economy with standard fiscal and monetary tools.

American corporate influence in Canada has spurred a variety of attempts to counter or regulate it. Under Prime Minister Pierre Elliott Trudeau, Ottawa established the Foreign Investment Review Agency and empowered it to approve or deny investment applications. In addition, in an effort to break the virtual hammerlock on Canada's energy resources by U.S. oil companies, the government has founded a state-owned oil company, PetroCanada, which has moved aggressively to buy out foreign holdings. Overall, however, U.S. influence remains disproportionately powerful in Canada—and provides a clear illustration of what European governments and corporations have struggled hard and successfully to avoid.

Meeting the "American Challenge"

In fact, the business policies of most European governments (and, in a different manner, of Japan) have aimed, since the early 1960s, at countering what then seemed a serious threat: a total U.S. multinational corporate take-over of the most important sectors of their national economies. For the Europeans, that threat was an especially daunting one as the logic of their new Common Market unfolded in the late 1950s and early 1960s. Not only were American companies in record numbers flocking to Europe to buy or build new plants, but the multinational arrivistes were far more adept than the Europeans at capitalizing on the Common Market's advantages. As tariffs and other barriers to the free flow of capital, labor, and goods among the six original Common Market members diminished, American companies proved agile at siting their plants where costs were most efficiently compensated for by cheaper labor, broader markets, or local tax breaks. But as the initial wave of post–World War II U.S. investment became a flood, European governments began to fear a kind of corporate conquest.

That mood was best captured by Jean-Jacques Servan-Schreiber in his celebrated polemic of the mid 1960s, *Le Défi Américain (The American Challenge)*. Servan-Schreiber argued that, taken collectively, the holdings of U.S. corporations in Europe by 1975 would constitute the world's "third industrial power," after the U.S.S.R. and America itself. He stressed that European governments and corporations could not simply ban the Americans from investing without setting off an economic policy clash that would shatter the Western alliance. Instead, Europeans would have to begin to think of their businesses in continental or global terms—much as the American multinationals did. They would have to study American management methods, and emulate the marketing and managerial skills that enabled the Americans to integrate production and sales across a half-dozen European nations. Because they had approached the Common Market in the same way they approached the integrated market of fifty states at home, Servan-Schreiber argued, the American multinationals had become the first true "European businesses."

Servan-Schreiber's call for a European response to the American multinationals was little more than a reflection of the entrenched attitudes of continental European governments. For decades, the rulers of Germany, Italy, and France had been deeply resentful of the Anglo-American dominance of the world's oceans. That strategic reality left governments vulnerable to blockade in wartime and to the menace of cartel prices for raw materials. (Most mining enterprises in copper, bauxite, and other minerals were, by the early 1900s, controlled by British or American firms.) Strenuous efforts by continental companies and governments to break the Anglo-American stranglehold, especially on world oil, had resulted in the creation of state oil companies in France and Italy as early as the 1920s.

Access to raw materials, in fact, was a major element in the most extreme drive of continental governments for economic autonomy—the German and Italian compaigns of conquest in World War II. Defeated and prostrate, the Europeans welcomed U.S. multinational investment in the 1950s for its role in reconstructing their economies. But the old memories and fears lived on, expressed in Charles de Gaulle's famous aphorism that the world was divided into "the Anglo-Saxons and the others." Given that background, Europe was ready and willing to cope with the American challenge embodied by IBM, Monsanto, General Motors, and other U.S. multinationals.

Ironically, though, the public awareness of the American

multinational "threat" to Europe's economies was heightened
by the reporting rules of American businesses that required
companies to disclose full and timely information on their sales,
earnings, debts, investments, and other key indices. The
strength of the European governmental and corporate response to the U.S. multinationals was, by contrast, mostly con-
cealed. For one thing, many of the largest European businesses,
like the sprawling holdings of the Flick family in West Germany, are closely held, very nearly private enclaves. Even publicly traded European companies are able to remain far more
secretive about their operations, finances, and investment
structures than are American firms. So the statistical immensity
of American investment in Europe stirred public concern, but
the growing size of Europe's own leading companies and their
widening global reach was largely overlooked.

In an exhaustive study, *The European Multinationals*, Lawrence Franko suggested that continental European companies
had, as early as the beginning of the 1960s, chosen the offense
as the best defense against the investment thrust of U.S. multinationals. After comparing the strategies of 85 leading European companies (excluding British firms) and 187 U.S. multinationals drawn from *Fortune* magazine's top 500 companies,
Franko concluded that, by 1971, "it was almost certain that the
rate of expansion of foreign manufacturing operations of large
Continental European enterprises exceeded that of large
American enterprises."

Throughout the late 1960s, when Servan-Schreiber's *American Challenge* was a European best seller, Franko's data indicate that companies from France, West Germany, Italy, the
Netherlands, and Switzerland were spreading a web of overseas
manufacturing and raw materials–producing subsidiaries
around the globe. Together with multinationals from Great
Britain, the total number of European foreign subsidiaries had,
by about 1970, probably passed those held by U.S. multinationals. By the late 1970s, the total sales by affiliates of foreign

(mostly European) multinationals surpassed those of American companies' overseas subsidiaries.

While the European multinationals were cross-investing heavily in the Common Market and venturing out into the Third World, their governments' policies in the 1960s were smoothing the way for mergers, joint ventures, and market-sharing agreements to enable national companies to grow large enough to meet American competition head-on. Thus, in the early 1960s, a wave of business consolidations swept the continent. As Ernest Mandel, author of *Europe vs. America,* noted, the most intriguing of these were the "transnational" links between large Common Market firms of different nationalities. In 1964, for example, the two largest photographic equipment–makers on the continent, Belgium's Gevaert and the West German Agfa, joined forces. Other mergers linked the Dutch steel trust, Hoogovens Ijmuiden, and the German Dortmund-Hörder-Hütten-Union; the French financial group Schneider and its Belgian counterpart, Empain. But despite these exceptions, the evolution of true transnational corporations has been slow in Europe. "To put it bluntly," British journalist Anthony Sampson wrote in his *Anatomy of Europe,* "companies in different countries do not trust one another . . ."

Within nations, European government policy also encouraged mergers of large enterprises to serve as "national champion" industries. In West Germany, Volkswagen and Daimler-Benz early reached accords on avoiding competition, and VW later went on to absorb the specialty car-maker, Audi. In Italy, the two leading chemical companies, Montecatini and Edison, merged, with state backing, in the early 1960s. (A decade later, Montedison would become one of the largest money-losers in business history.) In France, the chemical trusts Kuhlmann and Ugine joined forces. Later, with the acquisition of Pechiney, the firm became a true multinational giant (1978 sales: $6.6 billion).

In short, the trend toward larger, multidivision business concentrations, which had created the U.S. multinationals, was working in Europe in the 1960s—but with several crucial differences. Although U.S. companies had grown in a country traditionally hostile to big business (America had, after all, pioneered in passing antitrust laws), European governments actively fostered the formation of vast combines to achieve the economies of scale and research-and-development capabilities needed to compete with the American giants.

That sort of explicit link between government and individual corporations is alien to America's free-enterprise ideology (although, as in the case of loan rescues for Lockheed, and now for Chrysler, that ideology is changing). But European governments have long accepted their role as provider of support and guidance to their largest corporations. Cartels, market-sharing arrangements, and other anticompetitive schemes that would be illegal in America abound in the history of European business. So does the intermingling of government and private capital investment and the outright ownership of giant companies (Renault, British Steel) by governments. The United States has sought to maintain private railroads, airlines, oil companies, utilities, and other key industries, but European governments of both the right and left have not hesitated to nationalize industries that can't meet government goals by free-market means alone. France, Italy, and Germany, for that reason, had state-owned oil companies before World War II. Volkswagen is still largely owned by the Bonn government and the state government of Saxony.

What's more, European governments have proved ready and willing to fund the creation of whole new industries or projects. A striking example is the multibillion-dollar, government-backed joint venture between British and French aerospace companies that produced the Concorde supersonic transport. That droop-nosed financial monster may never yield a penny's profit to its builders—Britain was forced in 1979 to write off $320 million in loans to the Concorde consortium—but the experiment proved a prestigious technical triumph and helped lay the groundwork for later Europe-wide collaboration on the successful Airbus family of commercial jetliners. That sort of government willingness to aid, guide, and support national business proved a major factor in averting the much-touted take-over threat by American multinationals in the 1950s and 1960s, enabling the European corporations to meet the U.S. multinationals as equals in the global marketplace of the 1970s and to challenge them for supremacy in the 1980s.

But while European governments devoted billions of dollars and even diplomatic support to their "national champion" companies, the U.S. Government aimed more generally at structuring a world environment of free trade and capital transfers. Just as the Common Market's reduction of tariff barriers had made Europe attractive to U.S. investors, American global policy was conducive to the growth of all multinationals. In effect, Nestlé, Volkswagen, Imperial Chemical Industries, and Fiat grew under the free world political and military guarantees of the United States. European governments, meanwhile, focused not on general world business conditions, but on the health of specific national firms.

As a result, in the 1970s, U.S. multinationals faced larger, more efficient European companies, whose explicit aim was to break the near-monopolies enjoyed by American companies in nuclear power, commercial aviation, computers, and other advanced technologies. That "European challenge" matured at the same time as the resurgence of Japanese business—first in exporting, then in foreign investment.

Enter the Japanese and the NICs

Japan's rise, too, was largely a function of determined government aid and planning. Faced, in the years after World War II, with the collapse of domestic industry, loss of markets, and a rapidly rising population (much of it unemployed), Japan's postwar governments assumed a strikingly powerful role in the nation's economy. Government policy virtually banned direct foreign investment and discouraged Japanese businesses from investing abroad by imposing strict capital controls. Guided by policies that called for borrowing and improving on foreign technology, Japanese companies licensed U.S. and European experts in electronics, machine tools, and metallurgy. U.S. companies were naïvely eager to earn the seemingly easy returns from these license fees, and the Japanese were spared the overhead costs of carrying out their own research and development. In the long run, this strategy proved costly to the United States. It resulted in an inundation of large portions of the Western markets by Japanese cameras, tape recorders, motorbikes, cars, and ships.

For the first two decades of recovery (1945 to 1965), a labor surplus and the resulting low wages kept Japanese business eagerly investing at home with money borrowed from abroad and with low-interest government loans. Though its leading businesses thus became some of the most highly debt-leveraged in the world, Japan turned the corner into overall balance-of-payments surpluses around 1964. Because of the restrictions on foreign investment, the equity stake in that remarkable recovery was almost wholly Japanese. Foreign investment in Japan was negligible, compared with the U.S. stake in Europe or Canada. As late as 1970, total foreign holdings in Japanese business had reached just $540 million, roughly 0.27 percent of all industrial capital stock. Since Tokyo aimed to increase exports from home-based corporations, Japanese investment overseas was also marginal. Initiated in the late 1950s by government-sponsored resource-development projects in Brazil, Alaska, the Middle East, and Indonesia, Japan's total foreign investment was little more than $1 billion by 1966.

That picture changed sharply in the early 1970s. Japan's barriers to the inflow of foreign capital were slowly but steadily dismantled as companies like Sony, Mitsubishi, Toyota, and

Honda proved themselves able to compete on a global scale. But in the decade that Japan took to lower its capital barriers (1967 to 1976), the Japanese yen rose nearly 80 percent against the U.S. dollar. Foreign investment in Japan over the same period inched upward to just over $1.5 billion—still a trivial stake in an economy that reached a GNP of more than $500 billion in 1976.

But if multinational investors—both U.S. and European— were discouraged from investing in Japan, Japanese firms moved abroad into the new markets open to them with startling speed. Buoyed by huge trade surpluses from 1965 to 1975, the holdings of Japanese companies overseas mushroomed from $1 billion to $15 billion in a decade. Sony, Kawasaki, YKK fasteners (the world's largest zipper-maker), and dozens of others spun out foreign enterprises that have enhanced Japan's global economic clout.

The emerging Japanese multinationals have enjoyed firm government backing, in the form of preferential financing by Japan's Export-Import Bank and guarantees against losses suffered abroad. But like the postwar growth of the Japanese economy, the overseas expansion of Japanese companies has been carefully shaped to fit government policies. U.S. and European multinationals have directed most of their investments to advanced industrial nations; Japanese companies have aimed instead at the fast-growing economies of Latin America, Taiwan, South Korea, and Southeast Asia. Japanese companies are also moving aggressively to seize the new sales opportunities offered by the mainland Chinese. Japan's corporate presence in Asia has grown so rapidly, in fact, that it sometimes appears on the verge of buying outright the targets of Japan's World War II military ventures.

Because of all industrialized nations Japan is the most dependent on foreign supplies of raw materials and oil, one of Tokyo's chief goals has been the securing of access to minerals, commodities, and oil. Investments in primary industries—mining, wood pulp, petroleum, and others—make up roughly 30 percent of all Japanese foreign undertakings. Japanese mining companies tap coal reserves in Australia and bauxite and iron ore in Brazil; the state-owned Japan National Oil Company explores for crude in Iraq, Saudi Arabia, and offshore mainland China; the Alaska Pulp Company draws on that state's forests to feed the maw of newspaper and book industries back home. Japan's corporate quest for raw materials has managed to run successfully against the grain of growing resource nationalism, even while similar investments by U.S. multinationals decline. In 1970, the director of the Fuji Bank's Research Department outlined the drive's rationale: "The independent development of overseas resources has become an urgent matter for Japan. Europe and America have already established monopolistic market structures in essential resources, and the problem of securing stable supply at reasonable prices has become more severe."

Japan's concentration on investment in the Third World places its multinationals in position to capitalize on what are likely to be the world's fastest-growing and most profitable regions in the 1980s—some compensation for Japan's late start on overseas investments. Though their holdings abroad are still less than 20 percent as large as those of American companies, the Japanese multinationals are raising their stake abroad at over 20 percent a year, compared with U.S. multinationals' pace of 10-to-12 percent growth in foreign investments. Having conquered markets in dozens of countries, the Japanese multinationals have joined the pack of global investment competitors in earnest, and the yen's rise—like the powerhouse U.S. dollar of the 1950s—makes foreign investment ever more attractive for them.

Beyond the growth of Japanese companies looms the challenge of the newly industrialized countries (NICs) of the Third World. A number of these nations, especially Taiwan, Brazil, South Korea, Singapore, and the British Crown Colony of Hong Kong, emerged in the 1970s as the most rapidly growing economies in the world, with GNPs rising 10 percent a year over the decade. That explosion of output was largely fueled by multinational investment from the United States, Europe, and Japan. Textile mills, foundries, electronics assembly plants, and oil refineries were built by companies like Texas Instruments, Creusot-Loire, and Sumitomo. To all multinationals, the NICs offered cheap and abundant labor, political stability (often backed by authoritarian rule), and generally liberal regulations on capital flow, profit remittances, and tax credits.

But major changes in the heady atmosphere for foreign investors in the NICs are now shadowing prospects for the 1980s. Competition from plants based in these nations has almost wiped out whole industries (like the American TV-building plants of the 1950s) in multinational home countries. With millions of workers unemployed since 1975 in Europe and the United States, there have been anguished calls from labor unions and regional politicians for tariff and quota protection to preserve threatened jobs.

In the NICs themselves, governments have become more choosy about the types of foreign ventures they want to attract. The new cadres of the NICs' civil services are now often graduates of Harvard, the London School of Economics, and other Western colleges and universities. They bring home sophistication in dealing with the multinationals, and new concerns not heard of before. "We won't be the West's sewer," said one Malaysian official, discussing investments by businesses that cause high levels of pollution. Companies that fit the NICs' development plans are still very welcome; those that don't— like IBM and Coca-Cola in India—are asked to leave or sell out.

Unwilling to remain "branch plant" economies, the governments of the NICs are pressing hard to develop nationally owned or controlled basic industries—steel, auto-making, and raw materials–processing—to replace expensive imports and eventually to export to Western markets. Companies like Brazil's state-owned steel giant, Siderbras, are viewed by NIC governments as tools desperately needed to break the cycle of dependence on the industrialized world.

Building such projects can provide profitable short-term opportunities for multinational investors, but "those plants going up in the Third World are bad omens for the United States, the Common Market, and Japan," warned Robert L. Slighton, a Chase Manhattan Bank trade expert. Because NIC governments are moving steadily to demand that the multinationals transfer technology to their local employees, share ownership with local investors, and step up export sales, the wave of industrialization across the Third World poses serious—and potentially disastrous—political and economic problems for all industrialized nations in the 1980s. And for U.S. multinationals, it promises new and strong competition.

During that decade, decision-making control over the multinationals' subsidiaries in the Third World will pass steadily into the hands of host country investors and governments. South Korean steel, Taiwanese calculators, Brazilian petrochemicals, and a multitude of other products that have pushed their way onto world markets will imperil advanced nations' industries— even the home operations of the multinational corporations.

Yet if the advanced nations adopt protectionist measures to keep out imports from the NICs and more backward nations, two fearful consequences could occur. First, strapped for foreign currency and denied increased access to Western markets, the less developed countries could be forced to default on their loan obligations. The cumulative LDC debt had reached a staggering $250 billion by the end of 1979, and the specter of "domino-style" default would set off a financial panic, since much of the debt paper is held by Western commercial banks. Second, if the United States, Europe, and Japan don't move to admit more manufactured goods from the NICs, these countries could lead the Third World in retaliating. Their clout would be substantial, because the importance of Third World markets—and the scramble by the multinationals to supply them—grew enormously in the 1970s. Third World importers now absorb 69 percent of American rice exports, 65 percent of U.S. wheat, and 50 percent of U.S. cotton sold abroad. Third World buyers take 48 percent of U.S. electrical machinery sales and 44 percent of heavy industrial equipment. That could lay the groundwork for selective trade boycotts.

The industrial world is edging ominously close to expanded protectionism. Though the industrialized nations agreed in the latest 1979 round of GATT talks to lower tariffs between 30 and 35 percent over the 1980s and trim nontariff barriers to trade, no provision was made for admitting more manufactured exports from the Third World. Instead, industrial nations appear intent on wringing "voluntary" export-limiting agreements from the NICs—on penalty of outright quotas. Thus, at the start of the 1980s, political tinder that could ignite trade wars and a new mercantilism is being built up dangerously.

Taken together, the rise of the European multinationals, Japan's resurgence as an exporter and investor, and the dynamism of the NICs have eroded the status of American multinationals and pared their shares of the world markets. These forces have also cut into the strength of the American economy in the world. Some benchmarks of this relative decline were cited by Lawrence Franko in the *Harvard Business Review:*

In 1959, an American company was the largest in the world in 11 out of 13 major industrial categories, namely—aerospace, automotive, chemicals, electrical equipment, food products, general machinery, iron and steel, metal products, paper, petroleum, pharmaceuticals, textiles, and commercial banking. By 1976, the United States was leading in only 7 out of 13. Three of the non-American leaders were German, one was British-Dutch, one was British, and one was Japanese . . . Although the United States still had 69 (or 44%) of the 156 largest companies in the 13 industrial groups in 1976, that was down from 111 (or 71%) in 1959. The United Kingdom went from 14 to 15,

Continental Europe from 25 to 40, and Japan went from 1 in 1959 to 20 in 1976.

A similar decline has occurred in America's overall portion of world trade. From nearly 23 percent of all world trade in manufactured goods in 1970, U.S. exports (85 percent of which stem from the domestic arms of American multinationals) fell to less than 16 percent in 1979, a year in which the United States ran up a whopping $28 billion trade deficit. America's chronic trade imbalances since 1971 have, in turn, sapped the dollar's value while surplus U.S. currency piles up abroad. That has made the expansion of European and Japanese multinationals all the more easy. As a result, the share of American multinationals in total world foreign investment has fallen from more than 55 percent in 1965 to less than 45 percent in 1978. Over the same years, West Germany's share has nearly tripled, to roughly 8 percent; Japan's has multiplied fivefold, to over 7 percent; even the share of Swiss multinationals in total foreign investment has nearly doubled, to 9 percent. And that trend is continuing as foreign investment follows market penetrations by the world's most aggressive exporters.

Come the Revolutions

Sometime in late 1974 or early 1975, according to the best available estimates, the U.S. multinationals' share of total world investments dipped below 50 percent for the first time since World War II. That abstract statistical turning point becomes more intriguing in light of the other events of those years: the climax of the Watergate scandal with Richard Nixon's resignation, the final, harried exit of U.S. troops from Vietnam, and the onset of the worst business downturn in the United States and Europe since the Great Depression as quadrupled oil prices ushered in an era of slow growth and high energy costs.

The links between political events, shifts in the global balance of power, and the world of multinational business are neither simple nor mechanical. But both as a political society and a world power, the United States, in the mid 1970s, clearly passed through a crisis that rocked the confidence of the noncommunist world in its role as leader, undermined people's confidence, at home and abroad, in American government, and ultimately damaged the power of American multinationals. America's paralysis in the face of the upheavals of the late 1970s also undermined the investment confidence that had encouraged the U.S. multinationals in their globe-trekking growth.

In the half-decade that followed the collapse of the United States–supported Saigon regime, revolutionary movements backed by the Soviet Union and supported by Cuban troops and advisers uprooted the centuries-old empire of Portugal in Angola and Mozambique, heightening pressure on the white-ruled states of Rhodesia and South Africa (where U.S. multinationals hold a $1.8 billion stake). Soviet-backed coups installed what one writer has called "garrison socialism" in neutral Afghanistan in 1978 and in Ethiopia in 1974, after the pro-American rule of Emperor Haile Selassie was overthrown. In South Yemen, a Soviet-supported Arab socialist regime menaced the rulers of Saudi Arabia. Finally, in bloody insurrections that began in 1978 and climaxed in 1979, the Shah of Iran was deposed, rocking the American strategic position in the Middle East and triggering a second round of oil-price increases that hastened the 1979–1980 recession in the United States. Closer to home, Nicaraguan dictator Anastasio Somoza, a self-proclaimed U.S. "ally," was deposed by radical guerrillas and the urban middle class in July of 1979.

The most nerve-racking (and costly) of these blows for U.S. multinationals was the revolution that replaced the Shah of Iran, an eager customer for U.S. arms and technology, with an ascetic clerical government essentially hostile to the United States. American arms-makers, who had seen their overseas sales balloon to more than $10 billion a year by 1978, were deprived at a stroke of their largest single foreign client. Under the 1970 Nixon Doctrine, which called for the United States to arm and support "regional influentials," the shah had become a linchpin of U.S. power in the Middle East and a great customer.

Aswarm with arms salesmen and other purveyors of high technology, Tehran under the shah had become a virtual Mecca for multinational corporations. Lockheed, McDonnell-Douglas, Litton Industries, and other U.S. arms-builders had sold the shah more than $15 billion worth of tanks, jet fighters, destroyers, and rocketry in the years from 1974 to 1978. So when it burst —seemingly from nowhere—Iran's Islamic revolt not only wiped out a huge arms and hardware market; it also called into question U.S. policy itself. Armed to the teeth and guarded by Savak, the ruthless secret police, the shah's drive to industrialize Iran had seemed unstoppable. That it was halted, by a backlash against industrialization and all it brings with it, erased such prospects as Westinghouse's plans to sell Iran $1.5 billion in nuclear-reactor equipment—and also cast doubt on the future modernization schemes of other oil-rich nations and on the hopes of U.S. multinationals for a piece of that action, too.

The entire impact of the worldwide setbacks the United States endured in the 1970s cannot be measured easily on the balance sheets of American multinationals. But a broader, if less precise, analysis suggests that the perception of waning U.S. power emboldens foreign corporate competitors as well as revolutionaries, undermines the dollar, and compounds the Carter administration's difficulties in reasserting American leadership. For U.S. multinationals, those trends pose far more serious problems than the threat of communist insurgency or nationalist expropriation. That is because they are accompanied by slower growth in the world economy, political uncertainty, and, in the stark words of West Germany's Chancellor Helmut Schmidt, an intense "struggle for the world product."

More and more, that struggle is not waged only between competing companies jockeying for advantage in a free world marketplace. U.S. multinationals vying for sales, construction contracts, or investment go-aheads increasingly find themselves squaring off with competitors backed, financed, or owned by foreign governments. Yet the U.S. Government has no clear industrial policy at home, nor any intelligible plans for guiding and supporting American multinationals abroad. As a top officer of a major U.S. corporation put it: "A coherent national economic policy is not always easy to discern. Indeed, our regulatory policy varies from one sector of an agency to another, and from time to time as politics and policies change. This is certainly the case with respect to the transnational activities of United States–based companies . . ."

Hostility at Home

When U.S. Government policy toward the multinationals is clarified, it is frequently hostile. With scant consideration for the economic impact, U.S. lawmakers have reacted to the corporate scandals of the mid 1970s, mounting pressure from labor unions, and other political concerns by enmeshing the foreign operations of U.S. companies in a web of bureaucratic constraints. As a result, said a recent Conference Board study, "U.S. policy toward multinational corporations has become much more threatening, and many top executives in United States–based MNCs now feel that the policies of their own government constitute the greatest challenge they face in continuing—let alone expanding—their international operations."

U.S. policies appear to have been adopted without regard to changing conditions in world business. As the American military and political hegemony weakens and foreign governments press their companies' challenges to U.S. corporations, Washington has continued to tighten its regulatory grip. The astonished chairman of one U.S. multinational explained: "It's as if Washington thinks we're riding on top of the world. We're not.

Times have changed. The companies that are bucking us for markets around the world are getting smarter and tougher. And they don't have their home governments breathing down their necks."

By far the most disturbing government move for most U.S. multinationals has been the repeated attempts by Congress and the executive branch to use trade policy as a weapon in foreign affairs. Such manipulations began under the Nixon and Ford presidencies and have been extended by the Carter administration, which linked policies on nuclear proliferation and human rights to U.S. trade rules.

The first significant restriction came in the wake of Richard Nixon's 1972 visit to the Soviet Union and the subsequent declarations that the visit had opened a new era of détente. By 1974, after U.S. sales to the Soviets had more than doubled in just two years (to $1.2 billion), Sperry-Rand, Ford, Pepsico, and the Chase Manhattan Bank, among others, envisaged the growth of a huge new market for U.S. technology and consumer goods. On the Soviet side, the Kremlin was willing to borrow heavily and run substantial trade deficits to buy U.S. farm products, computers, oil-drilling equipment, and other goods. Soviet technocrats saw trade with the United States as vital to their country's economic growth, rising living standards, and, not least, as a way of building bridges to U.S. multinationals.

But because the U.S.S.R. lacked most favored nation (MFN) status in trade, Soviet goods that entered U.S. markets were penalized by an extra 40 percent tariff. While the Nixon administration sought MFN status for the Russians through Congress, it also pressed the Soviets behind the scenes to ease up on emigration of Jews to Israel, an issue that was politically hot in the United States. Dissatisfied with that low-key approach, Senator Henry Jackson (D.-Wash.) and Representative Charles Vanik (D.-Ohio) tacked on an amendment to the 1974 Trade Act that delayed MFN status for the U.S.S.R. until Congress was convinced that the Soviets would let more Jews emigrate.

The effect was to inhibit United States–Soviet trade. By 1976, it had peaked at $2.3 billion a year, and sales of manufactured goods had begun to fall sharply. Angered by the Jackson-Vanik amendment's intrusion into what they considered internal affairs, the Soviets cut back substantially the number of exit visas for Jews. Meanwhile, American allies, led by West Germany, vastly expanded their trade with the Russians. From 1973 to 1978, West German sales and contracts with the Soviets roughly tripled. Capping that trade drive, Bonn signed a ten-year, $20 billion trade pact with the Kremlin in 1978.

Under the Carter administration, sharp criticism of Soviet repression of dissidents further chilled the trade atmosphere for U.S. multinationals. In 1978, to penalize the Soviets for convicting a well-known dissident on political charges, the administration denied Sperry-Rand an export permit to sell Tass a Univac computer to score the 1980 Moscow Olympics. Permission was later granted, but the Soviets bought a French computer instead. Similarly, the Carter administration first approved, then delayed, then finally allowed the sale of a $140 million oil drill–bit plant to the Russians by Dresser Industries.

Throughout the 1970s, the on-again, off-again attitude of the U.S. Government toward trade with the Russians cost U.S. multinationals several billion dollars in sales—with little perceptible effect on Soviet policies. American trade restrictions against the Soviets appear to be the product of political grandstanding, not the result of an accurate assessment of U.S. leverage on Soviet policies. One top multinational executive scoffed: "These sorts of restrictions might have some effect if we had an absolute monopoly on things the Soviets need. But we're no longer the only store in town. We can cut off our exports, but the only people we really hurt are ourselves. Other nations are happy to get the business."

Similarly, as Arab nations stepped up their economic boycott against Israel, Senator Adlai Stevenson (D.-Ill.) attached an amendment to the 1977 Export Administration Act to prohibit

U.S. companies from complying with Arab demands. Under the Arab boycott, Arab League nations seek to bar companies that trade with them from doing business directly with Israel or with companies that trade with the Israelis. The boycott's enforcement mechanisms are very weak—generally little more than a signed statement of compliance. But under the Stevenson amendments, U.S. companies that sign such statements are subject to civil fines of $25,000 a year. It is hard to prove that the antiboycott rules have done much damage to U.S. multinationals' sales to the Arabs (or have been good at all for Israel), but the chief operating officer of a leading U.S. multinational said that "the rules are so vague that we've just had to forgo business in several Arab countries."

Yet a third round of regulations followed the Senate investigations that revealed the huge sums paid by dozens of U.S. multinationals as "finders' fees," or de facto bribes, to foreign officials to secure overseas sales. Under the 1977 Foreign Corrupt Practices Act, it is illegal for any U.S. corporation, its employees, or agents to make "improper payments" to foreigners to win business or influence foreign legislation. Corporations face fines of up to $1 million for willful violation; individuals may face up to $10,000 in fines and a five-year prison sentence. Despite pious codes of conduct passed by voluntary bodies like the International Chamber of Commerce, no other nation has passed similar laws restricting their multinationals' business practices abroad. Critics of the U.S. legislation argue that it makes it difficult, if not impossible, for U.S. multinationals to succeed in dealings in parts of the world where bribe-taking (and even extortion by government officials) is a way of life. Complained one U.S. executive, "In some countries, you have a difficult time importing your household goods, let alone starting your business, without greasing palms."

Unlike almost every other industrialized nation, the United States holds its citizens living abroad liable for U.S. income taxes on their foreign earnings. Until passage of the 1976 Tax Reform

Act, the first $25,000 of the foreign income of a U.S. citizen living overseas was exempted from U.S. taxes. The act lowered that amount to $15,000, though a special 1978 amendment added a series of deductions for extraordinary living expenses abroad, like English-language school fees. But on top of the inflationary impact of the dollar's decline, the increased U.S. tax burden has led to a wholesale replacement of U.S. multinational executives by British, Canadian, and other foreign nationals. "It is now hard to get U.S. staff to come abroad," said a multinational executive in Tokyo. "One extra dollar of tax burden makes us that much less competitive in the marketplace."

The Carter administration's well-intended campaign to promote human rights has gone far to erase the brutal image drawn of the United States during the war in Vietnam. But the means chosen to back the campaign—restrictions on Export-Import Bank financing of U.S. sales to countries that violate human rights—have cost U.S. multinationals hundreds of millions of dollars in sales without actually ameliorating these nations' human rights policies. U.S. antitrust laws, which have been invoked to prevent American multinationals from joining or cooperating with foreign cartels or market-sharing agreements, have proved a further, and unique, obstacle to U.S. companies' foreign operations.

The cumulative impact of these home-grown restraints on U.S. multinationals was summed up by Raymund A. Kathe, Tokyo-based senior vice-president of Citibank, and a veteran of thirty-three years in Asian business: "The Germans, the Japanese, the French and the British [multinationals], all of whom are advancing in Asia and elsewhere, are not bothered by anti-bribery and antiboycott laws, or by having to pay taxes on income earned overseas. These countries are laughing all the way to the bank." As seen by the U.S. multinationals, foreign companies enjoy vigorous day-to-day support from their governments in trade deals, export financing, and minimal bureaucratic regulation of their overseas operations.

By contrast, Warren E. Hoadley, executive vice-president of the Bank of America, lamented that "our multinationals get no brownie points from the State Department for getting a piece of the action for the United States." The head of a European subsidiary of a major U.S. car-maker added: "The French want Renault to succeed. The Germans want Volkswagen to succeed. The Italians need Fiat to survive, and you can see what the British are doing to save British Leyland."

The difference, in terms of penetrating markets, is an everyday experience for U.S. multinational executives. Royce Diener, president and chief operating officer of American Medical International, a small but highly successful multinational (1978 sales: $420 million), noted that when his company serves as project manager for hospitals abroad, "what normally would call for U.S. equipment is whisked away by the British and others with their attractive [government] financing plans." G. Robert Baker, regional general manager of Dow Chemical Japan Ltd., said, "Most countries have better export financing than American industry. And most foreign governments have ways of providing tax relief for exports."

The type of long-term, low-interest loans that are provided by government export finance agencies like West Germany's Hermes, Japan's Export-Import Bank, and France's Coface often provide the key margin of success for competitors of U.S. multinationals. W. Paul Cooper, president of Acme-Cleveland, a $290 million machine-tool company, explained why: "The [U.S.] Ex-Im Bank is a helpful vehicle. But it has to show a profit and pay dividends to the U.S. Government. The Europeans are openly subsidized in government financing. Our system just doesn't compare." In 1977, after months of negotiations, Acme-Cleveland lost a $28 million sale to the government of Poland because its 8.5 percent Em-Im financing could not match the 5 percent rate charged by European competitors.

In an ironic reversal, the availability of lavish export financing by foreign governments often serves to encourage U.S. multinationals to meet customer demand from plants in countries that provide easy, low-cost export credits. In Brazil, for example, 62 of the 100 largest exporters in 1977 were foreign multinationals, many of them American. To attract them, the Brazilian government provides near-total tax relief for exports, offers easy financing, and applies strong pressure. In response to the Brazilians' carrot-and-stick policy, the Ford Motor Company's Philco subsidiary exported $131 million worth of products from Brazil in 1977, many of them radios bound for assembly in U.S. cars. Philco imported only $66 million worth of goods, mostly components, into Brazil, for a net gain of $65 million for the country. General Electric Company's subsidiary GE do Brasil was an outstanding exporter in 1977, selling $3.5 million in refrigerators and opening talks to sell $20 million in locomotives to Mozambique. For GE, Brazil's export incentives made such sales even more profitable than exports from U.S. factories. But on the bottom line of the American trade balance—a key index of the dollar's strength—such sales do little good, and sometimes hurt.

To even out that sort of imbalance in export aid, the Carter administration's director of the U.S. Export-Import Bank, John L. Moore, has lobbied hard to increase the bank's maximum lending ceilings, lower its mandated interest rates, and increase its flexibility in financing the huge "spearhead" capital projects abroad that are the opening wedges for continued U.S. sales of spare parts, management services, and maintenance. Currently, Ex-Im must refer every project over $60 million to Congress for approval, a time-consuming process that gives competitors an edge. But though Moore has shaved Em-Im's loan rates as low as 7.5 percent on some projects and stepped up its share of financing from a standard 45 percent to as high as 85 percent, foreign competition often still wins out. On one project, for example, Ex-Im offered 100 percent financing to the United Technologies Corporation to cover the sale of gas turbines to Malaysia. Still, the contract was snapped up by a Japanese company employing a 4 percent, twenty-year government loan—a rate and term that Em-Im cannot now match.

"The Struggle for the World Product"

Beyond that sort of financial backing for their companies, European and Japanese envoys often appear to U.S. multinational chiefs to be carrying a sheaf of business deals alongside the dispatches in their diplomatic pouches. Trade-offs of political support, arms aid, or other government help in exchange for favorable deals for national companies are common. U.S. diplomats, by contrast, appear too preoccupied with politics to stoop to such mundane bargaining. One head of a U.S. multinational in Italy voiced his belief that "the Greeks bought the French Secam color TV system probably because the French government promised to aid Greece in its bid for membership in the European Community. No American government does anything like that for us. Our State Department people just don't think like that." To European and Japanese businessmen, in fact, "Washington seems more like an inquisition than a government," said a London-based senior executive of a leading U.S. multinational. Accustomed to hand-in-glove collaboration with their home governments, foreign businessmen can hardly believe Washington's indifference to the success of American multinationals.

The most bitter complaints about U.S. Government overseas interference come from multinationals in the American nuclear industry, which is still reeling at home from opposition by environmentalists and the public hostility caused by the near-disaster at Three Mile Island. "Our nuclear [export] policies," said Gordon C. Hurlbert, president of Westinghouse Power Systems, "have taken us from 100 percent of the world market to practically zero." U.S. reactor contracts won abroad have plummeted drastically to none at all in 1977 and just two in 1978.

The twin causes, Hurlbert charged, were the Carter administration's effort to limit the growth of plutonium-reprocessing technology abroad and its linking of Export-Import Bank financing to human rights issues. As a result, Hurlbert claimed, Westinghouse lost $1.7 billion in sales to South Africa, Argentina, and Brazil. "Somebody else got that business, though I'm the low-cost supplier." Nuclear export multinationals from France (Framatome) and West Germany (Kraftwerke Union) have stepped into the gap.

Equally bitter is George P. Shultz, Richard Nixon's secretary of the Treasury and now president of the secretive, California-based construction multinational, Bechtel: "There is apparently a perception in our government that individual trades can be turned on and off like a light switch to induce changes in the domestic and foreign policies of a host government. Increasingly, our trading partners see that we cannot be counted on as a reliable supplier." Nuclear plants all over the world, Shultz explained, "were sold on the express guarantee that we would supply enriched uranium to fuel them." Now, government suggestions that uranium may be withheld to persuade other countries to follow Washington's policies on spent-fuel reprocessing have caused "widespread resentment, even disbelief," said Shultz. "This is one of the ways our government has placed a chill on exports in general. Since the European, especially the French, are very much on the move in this area, the ironic result is that our influence—on the safe handling of nuclear materials and efforts to control diversion into weapons use—is diminishing."

Other once-dominant U.S. industries, in particular the aerospace companies Lockheed, McDonnell-Douglas, and Boeing, are facing intensified competition. The plans of European governments to build a world-scale aerospace industry grew in sophistication and success through the 1970s. The European consortium now building the A-300 medium-range Airbus is backed by massive subsidies, purchases by the government-

owned airlines of other European nations, and strong diplomatic pressures. The companies involved, France's Aero-
spatiale, West Germany's Messerschmitt-Bölkow-Blohm, the
German-Dutch VFW-Fokker, and Spain's Construcciones
Aeronauticas, envisage the A-300 as the first in a series of challenges to the American dominance of the commercial-airline
market of the 1980s. Dan Krook, marketing director for Airbus,
said that the consortium is aiming for a 30-to-35 percent share
of a multibillion-dollar market that now buys 90 percent of its
planes from U.S. firms. Because of the nationalistic pride, as well
as money, invested in the Airbus, "governments will buy it
instead of 747s, even if it's not justified economically," said a
U.S. multinational executive based in the Netherlands. "This is
a trade barrier virtually impossible for U.S. companies to avoid;
it's not like a tariff barrier you can jump with a new manufacturing site."

Similar government-fostered companies in weapons production, microprocessors, telecommunications, and computer
equipment abound in Europe and Japan, as these countries aim
to dislodge U.S. multinationals from the commanding heights of
late twentieth-century technology. In older, more mature or
stagnant industries as well, government-backed or -owned industries abroad pose almost insuperable problems for U.S. multinationals. Cheap steel from the mills of the British Steel Corporation, for example, helped drive the aging U.S. steel industry
into serious losses in 1977. U.S. steelmakers were simply unable
to match the prices BS charged to keep up production and jobs
even as its losses soared into hundreds of millions of pounds.
Such foreign pressure in all of the world's troubled industries—
steel, shipbuilding, textiles, shoemaking, and petrochemicals—
is unlikely to abate any time soon.

On the contrary, as the rapid growth of world trade and
economies from the year 1945 to roughly 1974 gives way to a
harsher period of stagnation, weak investment, and lingering
unemployment in the advanced capitalist world, the pressures

on governments to preserve jobs, prop up ailing industries, and lure job-creating investments has become almost irresistible.

Despite the fact that the latest round of GATT talks between advanced nations ended with a reaffirmation of free trade, a new and more subtle protectionism has emerged. Harking back to the once-derided theories of seventeenth-century mercantilism (which regarded a nation's trade surpluses and its holdings of gold and silver as the only true measures of its economic power), governments have moved away from the post–World War II effort, led by the United States, to create an interdependent world economy centered on the dollar. Instead of the quotas or tariffs that strangled world trade during the Depression, governments now rely on currency manipulations, cartel-like schemes, heavy investment incentives, a variety of indirect subsidies to exporters, and "voluntary" restrictions of imports from nations that threaten to disrupt home markets. Thus, the "trade wars" of the 1980s will be fought largely with offensive weapons, not defensive barriers. In Europe, Japan, and among the advanced developing nations, the goals are broadly similar: to maximize national trade surpluses and seek to gain as much control as possible over tight supplies of raw materials and fuel.

The trend leads—almost daily—to departures from the free-trade ideology and practice that the multinational corporations grew in. Here are some recent examples. In 1978, after Japanese car-makers had gained more than 20 percent of the British market (up from next to nothing in 1970), London bargained a "voluntary" restraint on exports by Honda, Toyota, Nissan, and other Japanese car firms. Throughout the 1970s, the United States has imposed similar restraints on sales of Taiwanese TV sets, Italian shoes, and South Korean steel. In 1979, when the Ford Motor Company announced that it was considering a new, $1 billion plant to expand its output in Europe, the governments of France, Austria, Spain, and Portugal entered a bidding war of investment incentives that eventually reached offers of nearly $450 million. In the wake of the OPEC price increases of June 1979, a horde of foreign ministers, national oil company chairmen, and President Valéry Giscard d'Estaing of France himself descended on the oil-producing states of the Middle East. Their goal was to secure for their nations or companies increased supplies of crude oil or expanded exploration rights. Several government spokesmen stressed their sympathy with the Palestinian cause. France, in addition, concluded a $1.6 billion sale of jet fighters and rocketry to Iraq. Gratified, Iraq raised oil supplies to the state-owned French oil company Compagnie Française Petroles, CFP, by 20 percent.

The competition to lure multinational (and home industry) firms into job-creating investments has already boiled into such fierce "investment wars" that Assistant Treasury Secretary for International Affairs C. Fred Bergsten warned, "There is a growing trend to manipulate the flow of investments and then impose performance requirements (such as mandatory export targets). This may increase the overall level of investment, but it may also produce a protectionist backlash."

Caught up in the increasing host country pressure to step up exports and employment, many multinationals may find it nearly impossible to maintain overseas branches in the 1980s. Those that plan to do so are working hard to tailor their production to fit host government demands. "In the good old days of healthy growth, about the only mistake a manager could make was not to expand," said Francis J. Fitzgerald, chairman of Monsanto Europe. "Now we have to tailor our strategy very carefully in order to find the right spots." Indeed, in June 1979, Monsanto announced that it would close its European nylon-manufacturing operations. Company spokesmen hinted strongly that the decision came about partly because government subsidies to fiber-makers in Italy and France had helped maintain persistent European overcapacity, which threatened serious losses for private companies.

In Europe, where the slow recovery of investment from the

1974–1975 recession has left unemployment hovering at record levels (5.6 million workers in the European Community countries were job-hunting in mid 1979), the trend toward "rationalizing" the continent's losing industries is well entrenched. Agreements to regulate markets and output in textiles, shipbuilding, steel, and synthetic fibers have been drawn up by the EC's commissioner for industry, Viscount Etienne d'Avignon. But U.S. multinationals that took stakes in these industries in their heady growth periods a decade ago cannot join such arrangements without violating U.S. antitrust laws. As a result, in part, U.S. multinationals actually withdrew more capital ($5.6 billion) from Europe in 1978 than they invested ($4.4 billion). Just over a decade after publication of *The American Challenge,* job-conscious European governments have begun to worry about a U.S. multinational retreat from the continent.

At the same time, in markets traditionally dominated by U.S. multinationals, foreign companies' sales and investments continue to outpace American companies. The most startling examples can be found in Latin America, but the pattern is evident elsewhere. "It's embarrassing," said the São Paulo regional sales manager of a major U.S. heavy-equipment supplier in early 1979; "I've made an informal survey, and I haven't come up with a single major industrial-equipment order going to a U.S. company in South America in 1978."

French, West German, and Japanese companies have taken much of that business, chortling over the U.S. policies that have made it possible. "Late in 1978, we were negotiating with Argentina to supply $250 million in generating equipment along with Allis-Chalmers for the Yacireta hydro project," said Robert Heinemann, Westinghouse Power Systems vice-president in South America. "Then the State Department bragged publicly about stopping the Ex-Im Bank's letter of intent for financing the project [on human rights grounds], and the deal was thrown open to all bidders."

Even where human rights–policy considerations have no impact, as in Venezuela, U.S. companies are meeting foreign competition backed by home governments, and often lose. A $250 million contract to build Caracas's first subway, for example, went to French contractors whose bid seemed "impossibly low" to U.S. executives. They believe the bid reflected heavy, though masked, subsidies from Paris. "We play it by the rules and suffer the consequences," said a dispirited U.S. embassy aide in Caracas. In automobiles, color television, and other growing business sectors in Venezuela, U.S. companies find Renault and AEG-Telefunken high in the running when the government screens foreign investors. U.S. multinationals still hold more than 50 percent of the foreign stake in Venezuela's economy, but their share is shrinking as European and Japanese multinationals strive for larger shares of the government's $12 billion industrialization program.

Elsewhere in Latin America, too, U.S. multinationals are losing their big head start to aggressive newcomers. From 1971 to 1978, U.S. multinationals' share of foreign investment in Brazil slid from 38 percent to 30 percent of the $12.2 billion total. "The U.S. companies aren't asleep," said the head of a European auto parts–maker based in São Paulo, "but they're being cautious, and the support they get from the U.S. Government is lousy compared with what we get."

German companies led by Kraftwerke Union have wrapped up the lion's share of Brazil's $15 billion nuclear-energy program and won a $1 billion order for hydroelectric equipment to be installed at the enormous Itaipu Dam on the border with Paraguay. French companies have cornered the hydro business in Brazil's Amazon Basin, and the Japanese are partners in massive bauxite-mining and aluminum-smelting operations in the interior. In Mexico, Latin America's other potentially gigantic economy, the U.S. share of total trade has fallen sharply, as the government, angered by the Carter administration's waffling on a major natural-gas pipeline and sales agreement, now clearly prefers to trade with or take investment from European and Japanese firms—unless a U.S. company offers a unique advantage.

The tighter market for U.S. goods and the closer screening of U.S. investments in Latin America show how close to home the global struggle for investment, profits, and jobs has come. Worldwide, as they head into the 1980s, U.S. multinationals confront more confident competitors, more savvy host governments, and the perception that their operations may be manipulated politically to serve some new policy in Washington. The decline of the dollar has even drawn foreign multinationals on an astounding shopping spree for U.S. corporate assets. Up $5.7 billion in 1978, foreign direct investment in the United States is now nearly $40 billion.

Yet for U.S. multinationals, the need for foreign investment opportunities remains compelling, if only so that they can stay abreast of the investment drives of the Europeans and Japanese multinationals. For many U.S. companies, foreign investments, whatever the risks, still offer far greater returns than similar investments at home. Besides, as one Grumman Corporation official explained, "You don't get into a poker game expecting to win every hand."

Despite the catalogue of woes described by their top representatives, the U.S. multinationals retain enormous strength. As J. Fred Bucy, president of Texas Instruments, bluntly put it, "The United States is still the world's leader in technology." That is true, at least in computers and their software, information-processing, telecommunications, and innumerable industrial-machinery categories. In addition, U.S. multinationals spring from a nation whose resource base dwarfs the bases of Europe or Japan. If, for example, the Carter administration's synthetic-fuel-from-coal program can be implemented without ruining the environment, America will trim its dependence on foreign oil more than West Germany or Japan can soon hope to do.

But even under the most rosy assumptions about America's

economic prospects, the U.S. multinationals, and with them the home economy, will have to transit a difficult decade in the 1980s. World markets will be marked by increasingly naked use of power by national governments to secure advantages for their respective national companies. If it ever really existed, the American multinational "threat" of global dominance has long been blunted by the successful growth of global competitors. U.S. multinationals will have to struggle in the 1980s for their share of the "world product."

If they are to win enough hands to stay in that global poker game, U.S. multinationals believe that Washington must design coherent and vigorous export policies that will match those of the competition. Except for sales of politically charged police and military hardware, they argue that Washington should abandon its futile, costly attempts to turn trade into a tool of foreign policy. Most of all, American multinational chiefs are eager to see some recognition from Washington that a nasty, neomercantilist world market is developing. If that trend can't be reversed, U.S. multinationals will need subtle but strong use of American state power to manage in the 1980s. Unless they get it, the erosion of U.S. economic power worldwide is likely to continue.

The Dollar

Crumbling Cornerstone of the Alliance

THE EROSION of the U.S. world economic hegemony shows up most starkly in the decline in recent years of the once-mighty dollar. The spread of U.S. investment around the world, the foundation of the American commercial empire, was made possible primarily because the dollar was the commonly accepted reserve currency of the international monetary system. As long as the dollar remained strong and at the center of the global monetary order, it was relatively cheap and easy for American business to invest and operate overseas. Just as important, a strong dollar permitted the building of military bases around the world at an acceptable cost to the nation and projected the power of the country throughout the international economy.

But by 1973, just as it was becoming painfully clear that the United States in Vietnam was heading for the most serious military defeat in its history, an equally stunning setback was under way in the lesser-noted world of international finance: the official dethroning of America's dollar. Although the dollar had been under growing attack throughout the 1960s, it was not until 1973 that the United States finally gave up all pretense of being able to defend its role as the central reserve currency of the industrial world by letting the dollar float freely against all other currencies. For the remainder of the decade, the dollar declined erratically but sharply, plunging the world into the most severe international financial crisis since the 1930s. As a result, the Western industrial world, dominated by the United States since World War II, has begun splitting up into regional economic blocs centered on such other strong currencies as the German mark and the Japanese yen.

The headlong diversification by governments, central banks, corporations, and private investors out of the dollar and into German marks, Swiss francs, British sterling, Japanese yen, and gold is rapidly transforming the international financial order into a multicurrency system rather than a dollar-dominated one. "We have noticed that when central banks add to their reserves, they do so in currencies other than the dollar, indicating their desire to diversify," said Alexander Lamfalussey, noted international economist and director of the Economics and Monetary Department of the Bank for International Settlements (BIS) in Basel.

The lack of confidence in the dollar is shared by borrowers and investors as well. The Morgan Guaranty Trust Company reports that the dollar-denominated share of total Eurobonds issued dropped to 50 percent in 1978, from 64 percent in 1977 and 90 percent in 1967. Mark-denominated issues increased to almost 40 percent of the total, from 23 percent in 1977; and various issues denominated in Swiss francs, and other foreign currencies increased as well. Although the dollar staged a recovery in the first half of 1979 after the massive rescue program of November 1, 1978, it soon faded again, and it remains chronically weak. At the same time, gold is quickly returning to its traditional place at the center of the international monetary system, with the Europeans including it in their European Monetary System (EMS).

The rise of a floating multicurrency reserve system is not new. It happened at least once before, in the 1930s, when British sterling was knocked off the gold standard and currencies began to float against each other. Unfortunately, that experience is sending chills up the spines of many central bankers, because then it led to a series of competitive foreign exchange devaluations aimed at gaining unfair trade advantages, and helped send the world careening into the Great Depression.

Nearly all economists agree with the conclusion reached by Charles P. Kindleberger in his famous book, *The World in Depression: 1929–1939*, that the last century has shown that an international monetary system dominated by one country and one currency tends to lead to a more stable world economy. During the nineteenth century, when sterling reigned supreme, economic conditions were relatively stable and world output grew. For most of the postwar period, economic growth also expanded strongly, this time under the United States–dominated system of fixed exchange rates that had been set up at the Bretton Woods Conference the year before World War II ended. By contrast, during the interwar period, Western industrialized countries suffered their worst depression in history, and the international monetary system was in a state of near anarchy.

C. Fred Bergsten's assessment that "it is unlikely that the United States can resume its hegemonial position of the early postwar period" is widely shared around the world. But what is most worrisome is that if the dollar continues to decline during the 1980s, the industrialized world could be in for a repetition of the economic and financial chaos of the 1930s. Certainly if the dollar weakens further, the competition among major currencies for greater influence in the world economic and financial system will become more intense. As the competition intensifies, efforts to defend or increase the strength of major currencies could lead to a greater rise in protectionism, with the major countries continuing to scramble to establish strong balance of payments by increasing exports at the expense of their neighbors.

Unlike the 1930s, however, when protectionist barriers were erected by individual countries, the 1980s could well see the emergence of large, inward-looking regional economic blocs centered on Europe and Africa, North and South America, and Asia, and dominated by Germany, the United States, and Japan respectively. And unlike the interwar period, protectionism will not rely on tariffs; instead, it will lean on subsidies to industry, on cartel-like arrangements like those now being constructed to shore up such weak industries as steel, textiles, shipbuilding, and chemicals, and on "voluntary" export-limitation agreements. "We are moving toward the emergence of competing currencies, and the question is whether we can organize it," said Lamfalussy of the BIS. "We will probably have to have regional groupings of currencies to organize a new international monetary system, in which case the problem then will be whether these become regional cartels."

The biggest step toward creating a regional currency bloc was taken by eight of the nine members of the European Community when they set up the European Monetary System in December 1978 and started it operating by the early spring of 1979. After more than a decade of unsuccessful attempts, all of the EC members, with the exception of Britain, were able to set up a system that will tightly link together their currencies within relatively narrow bands. It was the weakness of the dollar that provided them with the galvanizing force to accomplish this. The goal of the EMS is to establish within two years a supranational central bank that will be the next big move toward eventual full integration of EC member monetary systems and the realization of the ancient European dream of creating a single currency—the European Currency Unit, the ECU.

Realization of that dream is probably years away, but even now the EMS has added to the dollar's problems because investors regard it as a step toward stabilizing a number of European currencies and thus offering them more opportunities to diversify. Publicly, Carter administration officials applauded the EMS. "The EMS is a natural development in the evolution of the EC, and I do not think it is a step toward greater economic regionalization," Bergsten noted. Privately, however, administration officials have consistently worried that the EMS will hamper U.S. efforts to stabilize the dollar. What is more significant in the long run is that the mark-dominated EMS could become a competitor to the dollar-dominated International Monetary Fund (IMF), which has been the major institution managing the international monetary system in the postwar period.

The more the United States loses control over the international monetary system, the more difficult it will be for it to halt or reverse the relative decline of U.S. global economic power. A strong dollar not only once symbolized the power of the U.S. international commercial empire; it played a critical role in nurturing it. The spread of U.S. investment around the world by multinational corporations was possible largely because the dollar was made the key reserve currency when the international monetary system was set up at Bretton Woods in 1944 and brought into operation in 1945. As long as the dollar remained strong and at the center of the international monetary system, it was relatively cheap for American business to invest and operate overseas. But since the dollar began its decline in 1971, the cost of doing business overseas has risen dramatically, casting a cloud over the prospects for continued foreign expansion by U.S. firms.

The more the U.S. currency area shrinks because of a weakening dollar, the more the U.S. international business community is likely to have to retrench. Directly, the higher costs of operating abroad could force American multinationals to retreat back to the United States and withdraw from overseas. Indirectly, U.S. businesses abroad, particularly the banks that are located overseas to service the multinationals, will feel the pinch.

Already, corporate treasurers are doing more and more business in local currencies, which tend to favor local banks that do not operate under the same restrictions as U.S. banks. "The problem of the dollar prompted American firms to borrow funds as much as they can locally," said Albert F. Naveja, a vice-president of the Harris Trust and Savings Bank in Chicago.

"The corporate treasurer today is a sophisticated individual who has command of worldwide financing vehicles and the ability to touch world money markets instantaneously."

Similarly, the spread of U.S. banks abroad during the 1960s and 1970s was made possible because of the pivotal position of the dollar. Following the lead of American manufacturing industries, and primarily in order to serve them, U.S. banks used overvalued dollars to buy up banks abroad and to set up branches and subsidiaries. With the dollar the commonly accepted medium of international business, U.S. banks had a special advantage in serving both American and foreign multinationals. Ironically, the spread of U.S. financial power abroad was also greatly encouraged by the efforts of the Kennedy and Johnson administrations to correct chronic balance-of-payments deficits and relieve pressure on the dollar by imposing various exchange and capital controls. These efforts failed largely because U.S. banks went around them to tap their foreign operations for liquidity, and the Eurocurrency markets were the result of an end-run by the private markets around government controls.

It is ironic, too, that the incredible growth of the Eurocurrency markets will make dealing with the problems of the dollar even more difficult in the eighties. This vast pool of "stateless money"—which by some estimates amounts to $1 trillion—of course serves the needs of multinational corporations and other international traders and investors. But in the hands of the highly efficient international banking system and increasingly sophisticated treasurers of multinational corporations, billions of dollars can now be shifted around the globe with such ease that government authorities, especially central banks, are almost powerless to stop attacks on the dollar or any other currency.

Equally disturbing, the Eurocurrency markets, which now encompass Hong Kong, Tokyo, and other money centers in the Far East, can be used to frustrate national monetary policies. If the Fed, for example, wants to tighten monetary policy in order to combat inflation, U.S. banks can simply go to the Euromarkets to borrow the money their customers in the United States are demanding. Concern over these problems by both the Fed and other major central banks is not only producing demands for controls on the Euromarkets; it is also leading to more demands for measures to sop up large portions of the dollars in the pool. It is likely that sometime in the future a so-called substitution account will be set up under the auspices of the International Monetary Fund. This account will enable holders of dollars to turn them in for an asset based on a basket of currencies. Over the long run the United States will be responsible for taking unwanted dollars off the hands of the IMF, and that could prove an immense burden to U.S. taxpayers.

The rush abroad was so enormous that foreign deposits as a percentage of total deposits of the top ten U.S. banks grew from an average of only 6 percent in 1964 to almost 33 percent ten years later. By 1976, the average had jumped to better than 40 percent. But beginning in the mid 1970s, just as the dollar began to decline sharply, U.S. bank expansion began to slow while investment of foreign banks in America accelerated. Foreign banks were then able to take advantage of buying into the United States with cheap dollars, thus reversing the process. German and Japanese banks have grown so fast to keep up with their booming economies and the rapid spread of their multinationals in recent years that U.S. banks now account for only five of the world's top nongovernment banks, compared with eight or nine only a few years ago.

U.S. banks are also facing stiffer competition at home because of the decline of the dollar. Just as American banks flocked abroad in the wake of the vast investments by U.S. manufacturers, foreign banks in large numbers are now moving into the United States to serve their local companies. At the same time, they are competing with U.S. banks for U.S. corporate business. They have already revolutionized the way loans are priced in

The booming Eurocurrency markets...

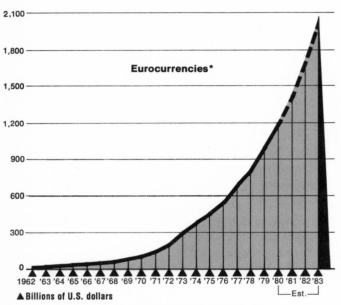

Eurocurrencies*

2,100
1,800
1,500
1,200
900
600
300
0

1962 '63 '64 '65 '66 '67 '68 '69 '70 '71 '72 '73 '74 '75 '76 '77 '78 '79 '80 '81 '82 '83

▲ Billions of U.S. dollars

└─Est.─┘

*Includes the foreign currency liabilities of banks in
Europe, the Bahamas, Bahrain, Cayman, Panama,
Hong Kong, Singapore, Japan, and Canada

Data: Morgan Guaranty Trust Co., BW estimate

this country in a manner that has simplified procedures and cut costs for many domestic companies.

For both political and economic reasons the trends toward a diminution of U.S. financial and industrial strength abroad and the division of the world into currency blocs will be difficult to slow or reverse. Maintaining the role of the dollar, or any currency, as an international reserve depends, in the final analysis, on economic fundamentals. The country with a reserve currency must demonstrate the capacity to grow solidly and in a noninflationary way. The reserve-currency country must also be relatively independent from foreign shocks, such as sharp rises in price or shortages of critical commodities like oil. Finally, a reserve-currency country must have substantial domestic capital markets that are readily available to foreigners. It must be able to export sizable amounts of capital and act as lender of last resort in a financial crisis.

By most of these standards the United States has been slipping, and slipping badly, for a long time. Although the American economy has grown faster than most other major industrialized countries during the seventies, particularily since the quadrupling of oil prices by OPEC in 1974, it has been at the cost of a severe worsening of inflation. And the price of getting inflation under control will be a protracted period of slow growth during the eighties. At the same time, the United States has proved extremely vulnerable to such international shocks as the hike in oil prices and other vital raw materials. And savings and investment in the United States, the main ingredients behind a capital market with breadth and depth, have been lagging behind those in other major industrialized countries, like Germany and Japan, for decades.

These are the fundamental problems that another Carter administration, or any succeeding Republican or Democratic administration, must come to grips with if it hopes to stem the decline of the dollar. But first, any administration must understand how important the health of the dollar is to the overall health of the U.S. economy and how this interdependence is likely to increase in the future. One of the most important economic lessons of the seventies was that fluctuations in the dollar affect not only the inflation rate, but the stock market, monetary and fiscal policy, and economic growth in general.

Unquestionably, the Nixon, Ford, and Carter administrations were made painfully aware of the ways in which a weak dollar could disrupt their domestic economic policies. But whether U.S. officials yet understand that domestic policies for the rest of the twentieth century will have to be tailored increasingly to international priorities, such as defending the dollar, is still an open question. It is generally accepted that "benign neglect," or letting the foreign exchange markets wholly determine the value of the dollar, is no longer an appropriate dollar policy. But there is little evidence that either the Republican or Democratic presidential candidates or their advisers have any well-defined active policy regarding the dollar.

The Politics of Dollar Economics

A continued decline of the dollar is, of course, not inevitable. Although no one believes that the currency can regain its former ascendency, the fact that the United States still has greater natural resources and a much larger self-contained market than either of the other two major industrial power centers—Germany and Japan—does hold out good prospects for halting the dollar's slide and even turning it around. Most economists, businessmen, and government officials recognize these basic facts.

The reason there is widespread agreement with projections like those of David Kern, manager of economic analysis at the National Westminster Bank Ltd., in London, which show the dollar continuing to fall against such weaker currencies as the French franc and the British pound, reflects a deep-rooted lack of confidence in U.S. leadership both in the White House and

Congress. There is skepticism at home and abroad about the ability of any administration—Republican or Democratic—to manage successfully U.S. resources, a skepticism that has been fed by the failure of the administrations of the seventies to pass an effective energy program. There is even greater skepticism that any administration can manage the U.S. political economy effectively enough to cut inflation and strengthen the dollar. "Over the long run it will be extremely difficult for Carter or any President to convince Congress, the public, and many segments of business that the United States must endure high unemployment, slow growth, and poor profits in order to help the dollar," said Ken Mathysen-Gerst, president of Capital International, S.A., in Geneva.

Such views are held almost universally overseas and are widely shared in the United States. And they are based on long experience with U.S. dollar policy. As far back as the late fifties and early sixties, when the U.S. balance-of-payments deficits caused a gold drain that first threatened the dollar, both Republican and Democratic administrations have generally tried to deal with dollar problems by stopgap, partial measures, without really tackling the fundamentals.

During the late fifties and early sixties, the United States suffered balance-of-payments deficits because government spending on military and foreign aid, and business spending for investment abroad, far exceeded what was earned from international trade and investment. In many ways the deficits at the time were unique. Unlike the classic case, in which payments deficits and a weakening currency are caused by an imbalance of imports and exports, the United States was running a balance-of-trade surplus. And unlike recent years, the country was undergoing inflation at about the same rate as other countries, and domestic economic growth was not strong.

At the time, many economists and financial experts believed the problems of the dollar were caused simply because the United States agreed to tie the dollar to gold when the Bretton

Woods system was established. Under the Bretton Woods Agreement, holders of dollars were entitled to convert them into gold at an officially set price if they wished. As balance-of-payments deficits persisted in the fifties and early sixties, many dollar-holders did just that, causing a significant drain on American gold reserves. Rightly or wrongly, confidence in the dollar and the Bretton Woods system itself declined almost directly with the drop in U.S. gold stocks.

The fact that the dollar was convertible into gold certainly did create problems. But the basic problem was the nation's balance-of-payments deficit. Whether or not the dollar was convertible to gold, a chronic balance-of-payments deficit was a clear signal to the world that something was fundamentally wrong with the U.S. economy. It highlighted the problem that the United States was living beyond its means and was not able to support its domination of the world economic order.

Dealing with such a problem is as much a political issue as an economic one. In the late fifties and early sixties there were very few macro-economic policy measures that either the Eisenhower or Kennedy administration could have taken to relieve pressure on the dollar. Interest rates were extremely low and in line with world levels. The federal budget was in surplus during most of those years. Inflation was low and showed no signs of accelerating, since the economy was weak for most of the period from 1957 through the first years of the sixties.

To defend the dollar, Presidents Eisenhower and Kennedy would have had to cut back on military and other forms of foreign aid and try to stop U.S. corporations from investing abroad. Eisenhower's secretary of the Treasury, Robert B. Anderson, did want to take steps to cut back spending in order to defend the dollar but was strongly opposed by State Department officials. Indeed, many of the European countries who were converting dollars into gold were not eager to have the United States make cutbacks in military spending or in other forms of aid at a time when the Soviet Union was still regarded as a major military threat. Basically, the Eisenhower administration dealt with the problem by expressing consternation with our former Allies for, as the administration saw it, their turning against the United States after all that it had done for them during and after the war.

The one policy that might have helped considerably would have been to increase U.S. exports around the world. No administration from Eisenhower's to Carter's has attempted to make exports a cardinal principle of government economic policy, although it is clear that revenues from selling goods overseas could support the dollar and buttress the U.S. presence everywhere. Ironically, a strong dollar in the 1950s and 1960s actually turned corporations from even thinking about exporting to concentrating on investing overseas. And today, with hundreds of billions invested abroad, many American corporations would have to compete with their own subsidiaries if they decided to export from this country.

This early form of benign neglect quickly turned into a more activist policy during the early Kennedy years. The dollar crisis had worsened when the deficit hit a record $4 billion in 1960. One of Kennedy's first major actions was to announce a program to eliminate the deficit, as well as to pledge to keep the dollar-gold relationship "immutable." At that time, gold was still $35 an ounce. Under Kennedy, the Federal Reserve Bank also set up regular monthly consultations with its major counterparts at the BIS in Basel in order to work out cooperative policies to defend the dollar. Out of these meetings came the swap line network of short-term credits extended among major central banks in order to defend currencies under attack.

But Kennedy's word and greater central bank cooperation were not enough to keep the strains within the international monetary system from worsening. In early 1963, the Kennedy administration took an even stronger step to reduce the payments deficit by promulgating the interest equalization tax (IET), which taxed foreign borrowings in the United States to cut back the flow of dollars abroad. Raising the cost of borrowing in the United States did discourage foreign borrowing in the United States. But it also encouraged all the big U.S. banks that were not covered by the IET to increase their overseas lending. This development greatly expanded the Eurocurrency markets, which many today regard as a major source of currency turmoil.

Kennedy's policies to defend the dollar and the Bretton Woods system, like those of his successors, failed primarily because they were in opposition to his domestic policies. At the same time as he was committed to defending the dollar, he was even more strongly committed to getting the U.S. economy growing again after years of stagnation. And he was also becoming more committed to fighting the war in Vietnam. Any administration that had persisted in pursuing all these ambitious goals simultaneously would have found that something had to give; eventually, it was the international monetary system.

President Johnson was every bit as committed to these programs, and more. Johnson, too, gave strong economic growth and low unemployment top priority. He was also committed to pursuing the war in Vietnam with at least as much vigor as his predecessor. And he compounded the basic problem by launching the United States on the most ambitious set of social reform programs in its history. The result was the triggering of an inflationary spiral that is still haunting the nation.

Not surprisingly, the U.S. balance of payments worsened as the sixties whirled on. By 1968, the country went into the red on the current account of the balance of payments for the first time in the postwar period. Until then, surpluses on the current account had offset a great deal of the deficit on the capital account caused by heavy long-term overseas investments by U.S. multinationals. The current account includes such major items as transactions in goods and services and government loans and aid programs. The deterioration of the current account in the late sixties was caused in part by a decline in the trade surplus, but mostly by the enormous pickup in government spending abroad due to the war.

Like his predecessor, Johnson attempted to deal with the balance-of-payments problem by trying to stop the leaks in the system with controls on capital movements overseas. He tightened up the IET in 1965 and added the voluntary foreign credit restraint (VFCR) program the same year in order to restrict bank lending overseas. But since the VFCR did not cover loans made by foreign branches of U.S. banks, the main accomplishment of the program was to encourage even more American banks to go abroad to service their corporate customers.

What the steady weakening of the current account balance was clearly signaling by the mid 1960s was that, for the first time ever, the pressures on the dollar were being caused by an overheating of the U.S. economy, a fundamental problem that has plagued it since. From 1962 to 1966, U.S. real gross national product grew at an annual average rate of 5.4 percent, well above the nation's then-estimated potential of 4 percent. By 1965–1966, the economy was running flat out. Unemployment had dropped to the lowest in postwar history; it was near the full employment target of 4 percent. Capacity utilization in industry was at record levels. More ominous, inflation began to accelerate sharply, a trend that has worsened, with only brief interruptions, right through today.

As early as 1965, some Johnson economic advisers recognized the dangers and began to talk of the need for a tax increase to offset the growing deficit on the federal government budget, also greatly swollen by war-related spending, and to cool off the economy. But no action was taken to raise taxes until 1968. As John Kenneth Galbraith noted in *Money: Whence It Came, Where It Went*, "To the natural reluctance to raise taxes was added the greater reluctance to increase them for an unpopular war."

This left the task of cooling off the economy to the Federal Reserve. With some reluctance, the then-chairman, William McChesney Martin, complied by tightening money growth and driving up interest rates. After a time these policies did help cause the "minirecession" of 1967, during which U.S. real growth slipped to less than 3 percent from about 6 percent the previous year. But even the minirecession did almost nothing to slow inflation and correct the basic weakness of the balance of payments and the dollar. Indeed, the economy rebounded strongly in 1968, and the current account swung into a $1.3 billion deficit from a surplus of about the same size a year before.

When President Nixon took office in 1969, he faced the same dilemma as had his predecessors: how to fight the war and keep the economy growing without pulling down the dollar and the international monetary system. By 1969, despite the 1967 minirecession, inflation had accelerated to better than 5 percent, more than double the rate five years earlier. But the tax surcharge passed the previous year swung the government deficit into a surplus for 1969. That, combined with another round of tight monetary policy, was enough to tip the country into a full-blown recession in 1970, when real growth of GNP declined.

A recession is, of course, a political liability for any President. Nixon in particular had always thought that the economic slump in 1960 had played a major role, if not the major role, in his narrow defeat by Kennedy. Thus, as the recession dragged on into late 1970 and early 1971, the Nixon administration became increasingly nervous about the presidential election of 1972.

As early as January 1970, Nixon reportedly ended the swearing-in ceremony of Arthur F. Burns as the new chairman of the Fed by asking him to "please give us some money." Although Burns has steadfastly denied that he ever bowed to White House pressures, and his bitter conflict with advisers H. R.

Haldeman and John Ehrlichman was front-page news, the growth of the money supply did accelerate sharply in 1970 and 1971.

No matter what the reason for the loosening of monetary policy, it combined with the phasing out of the surtax in 1970 to get the economy rolling strongly again by 1971. In fact, the economy started rolling at so quick a rate that inflation remained stubbornly high by standards of the day; it was about 5 percent. Equally bad, as far as the dollar was concerned, the deficit on current account, after improving dramatically in 1970, swung back into a record $4 billion deficit the following year.

When Nixon announced his famous New Economic Policy on August 15, 1971, it was clear that for the first time an administration was making some effort to grapple with the problems of the dollar as they directly related to domestic macro-economic policy. Indeed, the August 15 program was forced on Nixon in large part because of intense pressure on the dollar, which had been mounting since the spring. The wage-and-price freeze announced by Nixon was aimed at supporting the dollar, which was by that time being threatened as much by the divergence in inflation rates with major U.S. trading partners as by the perennial balance-of-payments deficit. And by cutting the "immutable" link with gold, Nixon set the stage for the first dollar devaluation. That took place formally at the Smithsonian Conference in Washington on December 18, 1971. Combined with the temporary import surcharge, the devaluation was supposed finally to solve the troublesome payments deficit.

Allowing the dollar to devalue was not only an admission that it could no longer be defended; it was also a historic departure in U.S. policy. Instead of attempting to maintain the dollar as the center of the monetary system, the United States would from now on follow neoclassical economic policies, which call for allowing a currency under pressure to rise or fall. In the case of the dollar, it was hoped that its decline would lower prices for U.S. goods overseas, increase exports, cut back imports, and correct the trade balance, which had for the first time since the mid-nineteenth century dropped into a deficit in 1971, joining the deficits in the current account and capital account.

Nixon and his advisers believed these policies were justified because they perceived the dollar as grossly overvalued. Such top Nixon economic advisers as Gottfried Haberler, Milton Friedman, and Henrik Houthakker, then on the Council of Economic Advisers, had long argued that the dollar was over-valued both because of relatively poor U.S. economic perform-ance and, more important, because of unfair practices by our trading partners. Until 1971 the Nixon administration was reluc-tant formally to devalue the dollar. But it was widely believed in the country and abroad that the administration policy was designed to force a devaluation of the dollar. If our trading partners were forced to accumulate more and more dollars as the deficit continued or worsened, eventually market pressures would force the dollar down or their currencies up.

Whether this was the Nixon policy by design is an open ques-tion. But the dollar was devalued at the Smithsonian Confer-ence by almost 14 percent against the mark and 17 percent against the yen, as well as by almost 9 percent against gold. The dollar remained fixed in value against other currencies. But once again, because domestic policies, such as the wage-and-price controls, treated only symptoms rather than fundamental problems, the dollar quickly came under attack. Primed by monetary and fiscal stimuli, the U.S. economy took off in 1972. Imports rose fast, and as a result the current account deficit set another new record; it reached almost $10 billion.

Such negative basic trends added enormously to the nervous-ness of the markets. Speculation against the dollar started al-most immediately after the Smithsonian Agreement as market players began to question whether the dollar was not just like any other currency now, open to continued speculative attack. These suspicions were fanned by the failure of the Nixon administration to follow through with any concrete actions. It was not until the summer of 1972, when speculation had again reached a peak, that the United States began to intervene substantially to support the dollar.

As always, intervention can buy only time. When Nixon removed wage-and-price controls in early 1973, inflationary expectations were raised and speculation against the dollar intensified greatly. By March 1973, the Nixon administration gave up any pretense of attempting to revive the old Bretton Woods system and cut the dollar loose to float—as it does to this day.

For many economists, especially such unofficial Nixon advisers as Friedman, the United States had finally adopted the correct policy toward the dollar. For monetarists and other conservative economists the float was the logical extension of benign neglect. In a floating system, balance-of-payments problems will be corrected eventually as the currency rises or falls as needed, so long as the proper domestic monetary and fiscal policies are also adopted. If a currency is weak because of balance-of-payments deficits and poor performance with regard to inflation, as in the case of the United States, the proper domestic policy is to tighten policy in order to dampen inflation. Because the depreciating currency should also be helping to correct the payments deficit, a government would not have to be as concerned about foreign economic problems and would be free to pursue the proper domestic policies.

The 1973–1974 oil crisis delayed the serious testing of this theory for several years. OPEC's quadrupling of oil prices came at a time when all of the major industrialized nations, having adopted expansive economic policies at about the same point earlier in the decade, were badly overheating. As a result, there were widespread shortages everywhere, particularly in commodities. Prices were already accelerating toward double-digit levels in the United States and every other major industrialized country in late 1973. OPEC was, in large measure, just jumping on the bandwagon.

By the first half of 1974, inflation was well into double digits everywhere but Germany, and it continued at that rate for all of 1974. Policy-makers, especially central bankers in the United States, Germany, Japan, and Switzerland, had already turned restrictive in 1973, when inflation started heating up in the spring. Burns tightened monetary policy early in 1973 and, with the exception of a brief period in early 1974, continued to tighten through 1974. At the same time, fiscal policy had been squeezed to the point were real government spending in 1974 was negative.

The other major industrialized nations also continued restrictive policies. In 1974–1975, with the business cycle already at a peak, the impact of tight policies helped plunge most of the industrialized countries into the worst recession in the postwar period. And just as turning expansive together in the early seventies had produced a synchronized boom in 1972–1973, the shift to tight policies in tandem in 1973–1974 led to a synchronized recession.

In 1975, real GNP declined in all of the major industrialized nations except Canada and Italy, and for the first time in the history of the Organization for Economic Cooperation and Development, real growth declined on average for all twenty-four members.

The recession drove unemployment rates in most heavily industrialized countries to postwar records. But it was also the chief reason that inflation in the United States dropped from 11 percent in 1974 to 5.8 percent in 1976. A similar pattern developed in the rest of the OECD as inflation decelerated to an average 8.6 percent in 1976 from 13.6 percent in 1974.

That was the last time in the seventies, however, that the major industrialized countries moved close together economically. The common reaction of these countries to the 1974–1975 recession was to adopt stimulative monetary and fiscal policies. But by 1976 most of the major industrialized countries, particularly Germany, Japan, and Switzerland, began to pull back when inflation started to heat up again. The primary exception was the United States, which continued to pursue expansionary monetary and fiscal policies well into 1978 because Carter and his advisers were worried that the economy's recovery would not prove durable.

As a result, the United States found itself in the late 1970s with many of the same problems it had had in the mid 1960s and early 1970s. The economy was overheating rapidly, and by late 1978 inflation was again heading for double digits. Concurrently, the United States swung from a robust $11.5 billion surplus on the current account in 1975 to a staggering $15 billion deficit in 1978.

Although the current account surplus melted away in 1976 and inflation began accelerating again that year, pressures on the dollar did not start afresh until the summer of 1977. It was not until then that the markets could get a really clear picture of the economic trends in the major industrialized countries. By then it was clear that both inflation and the balance of payments were once more deteriorating badly in the United States. Much to the consternation of the Carter administration, the BIS warned in its annual report in the spring of 1977 that if the United States continued to dump dollars on the world, a serious financial crisis could ensue.

That summer, Treasury Secretary W. Michael Blumenthal heightened that possibility by adopting a policy of "aggressive neglect" toward the dollar. Like many of the proponents of benign neglect, Blumenthal and other Carter advisers believed in 1977 that the problems of the dollar were largely the responsibility of the nation's trading partners. At the OECD annual meeting of finance ministers in June 1977, Blumenthal suggested that if the surplus countries—Germany, Japan, Switzerland, and the Netherlands—did nothing to stimulate growth in order to help America correct its balance-of-payments deficit, then the dollar might have to decline. Blumenthal and the Carter economic team apparently believed that if they threatened to let the dollar decline, the stronger countries would move more quickly to speed up growth and take on more of the responsibility as "locomotive" economies, along with the United States, to pull world economic growth.

For both political and economic reasons this proved to be a seriously defective policy, one that almost tipped the world into an international financial crisis. It is extremely difficult for any sovereign country publicly to bow to pressure or threats on matters such as the conduct of their economic policy, even if the pressure comes from the United States. Blumenthal also did not realize how deep was the fear of inflation in Germany and Switzerland and even Japan. Inflation was the number one enemy in these countries, and they were not about to shift quickly to highly expansionary policies, especially when they could see the damage it was causing in the United States.

As inflation and economic growth in the United States continued to move out of line with the other major industrialized countries, bankers, investors, corporate treasurers, and speculators became increasingly panicky about the dollar. For months, until the winter of 1977–1978, they had watched in some bewilderment while the dollar continued to drop. Since the dollar was still by far the most important currency in the world, most thought that it would soon stop dropping or that the United States and other governments would do something to stop its decline. It was still widely believed that the dollar was just too important to be allowed to go down and down.

Foreign central banks did try to stem the fall by buying billions of dollars in 1977 and the first half of 1978. The Carter administration became concerned by early 1979 and publicly pledged to intervene more to help prop up the dollar. The administration also began to take some steps to tighten policy and to make inflation its first priority.

The markets, however, began to demand more convincing evidence that the administration was serious about dealing with the "fundamentals," as Blumenthal labeled them. Despite administration pledges and actions to deal with the fundamentals, each month in 1978 produced more bad news about inflation and the trade deficit. Into the fall of 1978 the markets waited tensely for the long-promised new Carter initiative to fight inflation. When he announced only a voluntary program of wage-and-price guidelines, the markets turned thumbs down, and the dollar went into a tailspin.

The decline of the dollar quickly reached crisis proportions, and the Carter administration at last announced a program that convinced the markets that it took the problem seriously. For the first time in the postwar period, an administration clearly subordinated domestic economic concerns to the international problems caused by the dollar. Nixon had ducked the inflation issue by resorting to controls. Carter served notice that he was willing to risk a recession to defend the dollar. With many economists, businessmen, and government officials already worried that the United States might slide into a recession in 1979, the Fed and the Treasury adopted a deflationary dollar-rescue package whose main features were a sharp increase in interest rates and their pledge to continue to keep a tight rein on the rate of growth of the money supply.

The markets interpreted Carter's rescue package as a strong sign that the United States was willing to risk a recession in the year before a presidential election in order to fight inflation and defend the dollar. Carter reinforced this interpretation by presenting a relatively tough budget in January 1979. Backed by a $30 billion intervention package and the support of other major central banks to help until the fundamentals began to turn favorable, the dollar staged an impressive rally until late spring of 1979.

At the time, suspicions about the outlook for inflation and the balance of payments were again increasing because of the new hike in oil prices by OPEC, which was far higher than had been expected. Although the oil-price increases had a damaging inflationary impact on every major industrialized country, the

186   THE DECLINE OF U.S. POWER

central banks in Germany, Japan, and Switzerland tightened quickly and significantly in response. Interest rates were raised sharply, but with the United States heading into recession, the Fed hesitated, so U.S. rates were not raised very much. The foreign exchange markets responded by moving into strong currencies as the interest gap between the United States and Germany, Japan, and Switzerland closed sharply. The narrowing of the interest-rate gap not only made investments in German marks, Swiss francs, and Japanese yen more attractive, but it renewed doubts about the U.S. commitment to defend the dollar.

The Fed again moved to support the dollar. Chairman G. William Miller, as one of his last acts before becoming Treasury secretary after Blumenthal was fired in Carter's cabinet massacre in the summer of 1979, raised the discount rate by half a percentage point, to 10 percent, in July 1979. The fact that he raised the discount rate just as it was being announced that the United States had registered a sharp 3.3 percent decline in real GNP in the second quarter was again intended to underscore the intention of the administration to continue to fight inflation and defend the dollar, even in the face of a recession. Nevertheless, the currency markets continued to respond warily, and the dollar gained little ground.

The Dollar's Shaky Economic Foundation

The fact that the foreign exchange markets responded so tentatively to such an unprecedented move by the Fed illustrates just how suspicious the international business and financial community have become about U.S. policy-makers, the U.S. economy, and the dollar. By most of the important criteria by which a country is judged strong enough for its currency to be a sole reserve unit—inflation performance, growth performance, and independence from international economic shocks—the

United States is highly suspect. And the weakness in all these areas is in large part the result of more than two decades of unbalanced economic policy-making.

A succession of Republican and Democratic administrations and Democratic Congresses in the 1960s and 1970s, at a time when it appeared that the United States still enjoyed an unshakable preponderance of economic power, believed it was possible to finance ambitious social programs, strong economic growth, and the Vietnam War all at once. "The United States had to make the most basic economic textbook choice between guns and butter and decided to choose both," explained Assar Lindbeck, director of the Institute for International Economic Studies at the University of Stockholm. This mistake has shown up most noticeably in the steady weakening of the U.S. ability to control inflation. If the United States is unable to stabilize inflation, the dollar bloc will become a steadily contracting currency area.

Because domestic inflation weakens any currency as a store of value, the international financial community probably makes price stability its top measure of a currency's ability to play the reserve role. The protracted and steady worsening of the rate of inflation in the United States, compared with other major industrialized countries, is startling. During the first half of the 1960s, consumer prices in this country rose at a annual average rate of just 1.3 percent, compared with 2.4 percent in Germany, 2.8 percent in Switzerland, and 5.6 percent in Japan. In the second half of the decade, the inflation more than doubled in the United States, to an average rate of 3.4 percent, while it remained stable or accelerated modestly in the other countries that were soon to have key currencies. Worse, inflation was accelerating at the end of the decade in the United States while it was stabilizing elsewhere.

Inflation soared everywhere in the industrialized West in the first half of the seventies, propelled upward by the synchronized economic boom, commodity inflation, and the quadrupling of oil prices. On the surface, the United States appeared to have fared relatively well, as the annual rate of increase of consumer prices accelerated to "only" 6.1 percent, compared with 5.7 percent in Germany and a whopping 10.9 percent in Japan. But the statistics masked the facts that the United States alone started the decade in a recession that helped dampen inflation, and from mid 1971 until early 1973 clamped wage-and-price controls on the economy.

The degree to which the U.S. economy had become inflation-prone surfaced clearly in the latter half of the seventies. Inflation in America, as elsewhere in the industrialized world, slowed appreciably during and immediately after the great recession of 1974–1975. Beginning in late 1976, however, inflation in the United States began to accelerate and continued to do so until the end of the decade. During the same period, price increases generally decelerated in the other major industrialized countries until 1979, when OPEC again sharply boosted inflation rates by raising oil prices again. But when OPEC acted, the United States was much more vulnerable, because inflation had already moved into the double-digit range while it hovered around 3 percent or less in Germany, Japan, and Switzerland.

The worsening of the U.S. inflation rate in the late seventies was not only the result of the Carter administration's choosing to make growth its first priority while the other major industrialized countries targeted inflation as the prime problem. It also reflects a failure on the part of the administration to understand the economics of exchange rate policies. European economists, particularly Lamfalussy at the BIS, had long been worried about the inflationary feedback effects of the floating exchange rate system. Over the longer run, the depreciation of a currency is theoretically supposed to help correct the balance-of-payments deficit while providing the government with the time to put in place policies designed to combat inflation. In practice, however, the depreciation of a currency has tended to feed inflation, especially in smaller economies heavily dependent on imports. In the short run, a weakening currency can greatly complicate the life of policy-makers by pressuring them to adopt politically unpopular restrictive measures quickly in order to fight inflation.

Conversely, an appreciating currency can greatly help countries with a balance-of-payments surplus. Although the strengthening currency will eventually hurt exports from the country with a surplus, there may be a considerable time lag if the stronger currency helps keep costs down by cheapening imports. This is what happened in the case of Germany, Japan, and Switzerland, as well as some other industrialized countries. The sharp rise of the mark, the franc, and the yen cut the costs of imports, especially of such important dollar-denominated imports as oil, and the slowing of overall production costs more than offset the loss of price competitiveness in world markets due to the rise in export prices. As a result, the steep appreciation of the mark, the franc, and the yen in 1977 and 1978 hardly made a dent in the large payments surpluses of Germany, Switzerland, and Japan.

Until late 1978, Carter administration advisers, as well as a majority of American economists, believed that the United States was immune from such "vicious and virtuous" cycles. Because the United States is a relatively self-contained economy and is much less dependent on foreign trade than other major industrialized countries, with imports accounting for less than 8 percent of the GNP, compared with 20 to 30 percent in most other countries, a sharp decline in the dollar was not expected to have a great impact on inflation. Such an analysis overlooked the fact that a large proportion of American imports are critical materials and that a sharp rise in price resulting from a fall in the dollar can have wide-reaching inflationary consequences. Calculations by Data Resources, Incorporated, indicate that a 10 percent devaluation of the dollar can add as much as 2 percent to the consumer price index within two years.

The other flaw in the analysis of Carter's advisers was that devaluing the dollar at a time when the economy was near its peak could fan inflationary expectations and further strain capacity. To the extent that the cheaper dollar increased demand for U.S. exports, it also increased demand for factors of production that were already scarce, thus adding to cost pressures. The raising of inflationary expectations at a time when the dollar was under pressure of course added further to its problems. "We forgot another Economics 101 rule, that you do not devalue a currency when the economy is near to or running at full capacity," noted an economist with the U.S. delegation to the OECD.

By late 1978 the United States was in a vicious cycle. Each monthly announcement of a worsening in inflation pushed the dollar down more. At the same time, the decline of the dollar was feeding inflation and inflationary expectations. "The November 1, 1978, package to rescue the dollar was of enormous significance because it reflected the clear recognition in the administration that excessive depreciation of the dollar was not only harmful to the international financial markets but directly harmful to the U.S. economy," conceded an administration official at the time.

Many economists believe that it is far more than just the vagaries of short-term macro-economic policies that are the major cause of the U.S. inflation and dollar problems. Throughout its history, the United States, because of its enormous resources, had been able to provide its citizens with a steadily rising standard of living that has been among the highest in the world for the past 200 years. Convincing the public that its standard of living must stop rising as fast, or even decline, because it is helping to fuel inflation and weaken the country's international economic position would be an extremely difficult political task.

"An economy becomes inflation-prone when its government becomes weaker and cannot deliver all that the people want," said Patrick Minford, an economist at the University of Liverpool. "In the case of the United States, which has an economic empire, it becomes an especially severe problem, since it has big international projects as well as domestic projects to finance. When it is no longer possible to finance these projects with tax revenues, the government unfortunately simply prints more money."

Delivering all that the people want is going to become a more and more difficult problem for any President. The inflation problem in the United States has become so severe that probably only another severe recession followed by a protracted period of slow growth will dampen it significantly. The history of the past decade shows that at the end of each business cycle inflation has moved up to a higher plateau. The 1967 minirecession barely held inflation to around 3 percent, and during the next three years of recovery the rate of price increases rapidly accelerated to around 6 percent. The mild recession of 1970 cut the rate of inflation from 6 percent to around 4 percent, but without controls inflation would have surged again, as it did when the controls were removed in 1973. Even the severe recession of 1974–1975, which lasted about six quarters in the United States, was able to cut the underlying inflation rate to only about 6 percent, from its peak of better than 12 percent.

With inflation running at 14 percent at the height of the latest business cycle in early 1979, it is obvious that "wringing out" inflation could require the most drawn-out, costly economic slow-down of the postwar period. The only alternative would be to impose wage-and-price controls once more. But the disastrous failure of the Nixon program makes it highly unlikely that labor, business, or government officials would choose that route again.

A long spell of slow economic growth could have a mixed impact on the dollar if it dampens inflation. But historically, countries and investors have not been willing to hold balances in a currency that is backed by a secularly weak economy. The

fact that the United States, alone among the major industrialized countries, has had to put its economy through a recession
three times in the seventies in order to fight inflation has raised
serious doubts about its long-run growth prospects.

The widespread consensus among U.S. economists that the
potential growth rate of the United States will decline in the
eighties has added to these concerns. In one recent annual
report to the President, the Council of Economic Advisers estimated that, because of a continued slowing of the growth rate
of productivity, the most that the U.S. economy could grow
without generating inflation was about 3.3 percent, compared
with almost 4 percent during most of the postwar period.
Slower growth of productivity will also make it difficult to control inflation if workers insist on large wage gains, as they have
in recent years in order to stay at least abreast of inflation.

A satisfactory explanation for the marked slowing in U.S. productivity growth is still to be discovered by economists. It is
equally unclear why productivity still gains in Germany and
Japan, which are past the recovery and catch-up stages, following the devastation of the war, when rapid productivity growth
would be expected. What is clear is that if the divergent trends
in productivity performance continue, there will be even more
problems for the dollar and the U.S. global economic role.

The growing dependence of the United States on world markets and on a whole range of such imported commodities as oil
will also make it difficult to control inflation and set the economy on a stable growth path. The explosion of commodity
prices in 1972–1973, apart from oil, added enormously to U.S.
inflation problems. In 1979, the decision by OPEC to let prices
rise by as much as 50 percent on average, rather than the 14
percent expected by the administration, completely disrupted
economic policy-making. Higher oil prices meant not only
more inflation but a more severe balance-of-payments deficit.
This, in turn, meant that America would have to endure higher
interest rates longer than expected even though the economy

was sinking into recession. The freedom of the Fed to loosen policy in response to the recession was largely circumscribed by fear of the impact such a loosening would have on the dollar.

A study by the Federal Reserve Bank of Dallas in late 1978 showed that, though the United States is still the least open of all major industrialized countries—that is, it is still the least affected by international economic developments—its vulnerability to international shocks increased far more rapidly during the seventies than that of any other country. This reflects, in large measure, the growing dependence of the United States on exports. During the seventies, exports as a percentage of GNP grew sharply. More than ever, major U.S. companies are dependent on the growth of world trade and their ability to compete in world markets.

The Realpolitik of Currency Blocs

Because of the relative decline of the American economy in the world and the coincident rise of economic power blocs in Europe and Asia, it will become increasingly difficult for the United States to remain independent in the 1980s. The United States has neither the means nor the desire to make Europe and Japan prostrate.

As long as U.S. power was lopsidedly dominant, other countries were forced to hold more dollars than they liked. During the early postwar period, they benefited from an overvalued dollar; it made it easier for them to sell to the United States, which until the early sixties was by far the most affluent market for the heavily export-oriented Europeans and Japanese. For Germany and Japan in particular, the access to the U.S. market was critically important to their efforts to build up export-based economies. Both countries hoped that by closely linking themselves economically to their former adversaries, they would both resurrect their economies and also prevent future wars.

The United States, of course, strongly supported both those aims.

The November 1, 1978, dollar-rescue package represented a major turning point in U.S. economic relations with the rest of the world. For the first time in the postwar period, the other major industrialized countries made it clear that they could not and would not passively accept ever greater numbers of dollars. Moreover, they had become economically strong enough and sufficiently independent to force the United States to do their bidding. The Carter administration had begun its term in office by trying to force America's trading partners, especially Germany and Japan, to adopt policies to make their economies grow faster in order to help the dollar. By the end of the term, Carter was forced to follow the policy dictates of the major industrial countries that the United States accept a recession.

A major reason for this change is that neither Europe nor Japan is as dependent on the U.S. market as it once was. Chiefly because of the success of the EC in creating a large integrated market in Europe, U.S. exports to the nine members have declined steeply between 1957 and 1980. At the same time, intra-EC trade has more than doubled. Similarly, Japan's trade with Europe and the less developed countries accounts for a larger and larger share of total exports. Thus, the fear of a recession in the United States pulling everyone else down, as it did during most of the postwar period, is no longer a great concern to other major industrialized countries.

European and Japanese influence on U.S. policy-making will probably grow during the eighties. The EMS was set up mainly to protect Europe from the instability caused by the weak dollar. So far, the EMS has achieved that purpose. And as long as the other Europeans are willing to follow Germany's lead in fighting inflation, the mark and other EMS currencies will become increasingly attractive alternatives to the dollar.

By the end of the seventies many bankers and other market players were convinced that the Bundesbank, or German central bank, and the Bank of Japan had as much control over the fate of the dollar as did Washington. "If the Bundesbank says it will not defend the dollar, then any U.S. government will have serious problems," noted Kees Scholtes, an economist with the Chemical Bank in Brussels. A dramatic example of the growing vulnerability of U.S. policy to foreign influence occurred in the spring and summer of 1979, when the unexpectedly sharp rise in German interest rates, caused by the Bundesbank's tight anti-inflation policy, forced the Fed to raise interest rates even while the economy was sinking into recession.

The difficult experiences of both Britain and the United States as reserve-currency countries have made Germany and Japan cautious about pursuing the role for themselves. Inexorably, a reserve currency tends to become overvalued as demand increases for it both as an investment vehicle and for trade. This trend toward overvaluation is heightened by the reluctance of a reserve-currency government to alter the currency's value as well as by the government's penchant for adopting relatively inflationary policies.

An overvalued currency, of course, makes buying up assets around the globe an inexpensive venture. But it can also lead to a steady deterioration of the reserve currency's competitiveness in world trade, as the American and British cases illustrate. Both Germany and Japan are far more dependent than the United States on trade, and their governments and export industries have long resisted the drift toward becoming reserve-currency countries.

But that drift will be difficult to reverse. Efforts by German authorities to control the expansion of the mark's role in the Eurocurrency market and as an increasing part of the central bank's reserves have been no more successful than similar efforts to control international capital flows by the United States in the 1960s. New controls, like those proposed by the United States, which call for reserve requirements on Eurocurrency markets, are also unlikely to work. A major reason is that large money-center countries, such as Britain and Switzerland, which greatly profit from their roles as international money turn-tables, will not cooperate. Indeed, German multinational bank-ers, who are now almost as important as their London counter-parts, also do not want their lucrative international activities curtailed.

It is not just profit-minded bankers who see advantages in the mark and yen becoming reserve units. Both German and Japa-nese manufacturing corporations have invested billions in the United States in recent years in order to take advantage of the cheap dollar, just as their U.S. counterparts did the same abroad in the 1950s and 1960s. And some government authorities and politicians in both countries recognize that being a reserve-currency nation means increased political and economic power. Strong currency areas grouped around Germany and Japan will, for example, make these countries attractive to OPEC investors, whose confidence in the dollar has been ir-reparably damaged. That, in turn, could enhance the ability of Europe and Japan to compete with the United States for Mid-east oil.

Historically, the emergence of national or regional economic power centers has had a large political dimension. The spread of mercantilism in the seventeenth and eighteenth centuries is often credited with contributing significantly to the emergence of the European nation-states. Similarly, the neomercantilist policies cropping up in Europe and Japan today could serve to help create regional economic power blocs.

The trend toward currency blocs is likely to continue no matter what happens to the dollar. Some relative decline of U.S. economic power was perhaps inevitable in recent years. "When new large economic powers, such as Germany and Japan, emerge there will be a grouping of some economies around them," noted Professor Harold R. Rose, group economic adviser for Barclays Bank Ltd. "There would have been a mark bloc even if the dollar had no problems, because the Benelux and

Scandinavian countries are naturally very economically dependent on Germany."

But how well the United States manages the dollar will be critically important in determining just how powerful these alternative currency blocs become and how orderly is the evolution to a multireserve-currency world. More than ever, the United States will have to cooperate with other major industrialized countries to fight against the drift toward protectionism, which could end by pitting the major economic power centers against one another in a replay of the 1930s. Equally important, the U.S. Government must understand that the health of the dollar depends, in the final analysis, on stable, noninflationary growth of the economy. The lesson of the seventies for the United States is that it cannot have one without the other. It took almost the whole decade of the seventies for American policy-makers and the public to begin to appreciate the severity of the energy crisis. It is unlikely that the financial markets will provide the United States that much time during the eighties to understand that a continued dollar crisis could be equally serious.

Policy
Prescriptions

REVERSING THE DECLINE of U.S. power in the decade ahead will be one of the most difficult tasks ever undertaken by the nation. The decline clearly ranks as a crucial disjuncture, one that will determine the country's future for the rest of the twentieth century and beyond. The response to the U.S. fall from global supremacy will affect Americans in the most personal ways possible. Already the decline has raised the prices they pay for housing and food and for the kinds of cars they drive. It will go much further in the 1980s and influence the country's entire standard of living and even its security. Just as history tolls the names of past world powers that now rank as third-rate countries, from Portugal and Spain to China and even Britain, so, too, may the United States join that list unless the nation sharply changes its present course.

To stop the erosion of U.S. power, the country and its leadership in Washington must first realize that the economic welfare of the United States now depends on how America operates in the international arena. The major problems afflicting the country are all linked together. Their common cause is a fundamentally weak economy that simply cannot compete effectively and pay its own way among the nations of the world. Unless that economy is made more productive, and the goods it makes become more attractive and less costly on the international markets, the country will continue to suffer.

What is needed today as a first step is a redefinition of the role of the United States and its place within the global arena. For about twenty-five years, from the end of World War II to the early 1970s, the United States was clearly superior in both economic and military might to any single country or combination of countries around the world. In the last decade, however, the relative power of the United States has declined tremendously while the economic and political influence of other nations has improved sharply. The United States has become just one strong player—albeit still the strongest—among several very powerful players. But though America continues to play by the old rules of the game, those rules are now working to its distinct disadvantage.

The world economic order built by the United States after World War II has long since faded away. While America was concentrating on defending the open economic system from external and internal enemies, other nations began changing the rules of the game. In the late 1960s and early 1970s, while the United States spent its energy and power on fighting a proxy war in Vietnam against Russian and Chinese communism, other countries within the global economy started shifting their policies in radically different ways, and these policies now threaten the free trade and capital flow ideals of the postwar era.

OPEC created an energy cartel, and neomercantilist trade policies took effect in Europe and Japan. While the U.S. market remained open to the products and investments of other countries to an unprecedented degree, Japan remained closed and Europe began to cartelize its industries. Government subsidies to local corporations in Europe have become common as the governments attempt to lower unemployment and aid exports. Currency manipulation is being practiced, and capital controls are going up. The United States assumed that while it kept its eye on defending the system, the system would remain open. It didn't, and the United States has been caught short, without any new effective economic or political policies. In fact, the only response by America to date—and a pathetic one it is—has been to retaliate with protectionist actions of its own for steel, textiles, TVs, and shoes.

Europe and Japan have shifted from being cooperative dependents of the United States to aggressive competitors for markets, energy sources, raw materials, and political influence around the world. They are moving away from the United States to enter into their own alliances with OPEC oil exporters and Third World technology importers. They are trading heavily with eastern Europe and the Soviet Union while the United States holds back. In addition, while the major industrialized countries of the West are turning away from the United States, the former less developed countries of Asia and Latin America are transforming themselves into the newly industrialized countries of the world. They are moving from mendicant satellites of America to strong economic challengers in the global trade markets. The final change in the U.S. decline of power is in its relations with the Soviet Union. The military superiority that once defined U.S. ties with the Soviet Union has given way to a shaky parity, with all the doubts and dangers the shift involves.

America must not only redefine its vital national interests overseas; it must narrow them. It is no longer enough to mindlessly focus on the Soviet Union as a military enemy while the economic heart of the country is being eaten away by other nations. The Soviet Union is not putting a cap on the amount of energy the United States is being allowed to import; OPEC is doing that. The Soviet Union is not fighting for every overseas market and every source of raw materials that exist around the world; America's political allies in Europe and Japan are doing that. In short, the country can no longer ignore its economic interests abroad. It must return to the pragmatism of the Yankee traders, who cared less for ideology than for profits. If it was ever proper for the United States to take on itself the role of spreading democracy around the world, it is no longer strong enough even to consider such a role.

More than that, the United States is passing through a period where a fascination with the inner mind and the ego have replaced a concern for the outer realities of the practical world. Individual feelings and experiences are the primary concerns of people who are strongly antagonistic toward science and technology. There is a "greening" of American attitudes by many who seek a return to an imaginary bucolic, simpler time.

Those seeking the greening of America's mentality are joined by groups seeking the "pastoralizing" of America's economy. Environmentalists have shown themselves to be as narrow-minded as the industrialists they condemn. Just as corporations failed stupidly for years to take into account what their manufacturing operations were doing to the air, water, and land, so do the environmentalists now completely disregard what their demands and regulations are doing to the economy. There is a cost to cleaning up the environment in terms of production, jobs, and inflation, but there is no room in the environmentalists' arguments for that price. In fact, they have also shown a strong tendency to believe in an end to all growth and a return to some mythical agricultural society where life is uncomplicated and all birds sing.

There is no doubt that private industry in the United States for decades knowingly polluted the environment without any regard for the people living in it. The sad example of the Hooker Chemicals and Plastics Corporation, a subsidiary of Occidental Petroleum, is a perfect case in point. Hooker officials realized several decades ago that they were dumping dangerous chemicals into the Love Canal in Niagara Falls, New York, and did nothing about it. In fact, they denied to the government any knowledge about it. Had Hooker notified the authorities anywhere along the line over those long decades, steps could have been taken to contain the chemicals, and public anger against all chemical companies might have been averted. Businessmen complaining about the widespread public dislike of business can blame only themselves for this incident. Yet many

environmentalists have used this example to call for the stopping of *all* production of chemicals.

But what has made America strong until a few years ago has
been a drive to produce more—not less. It has been powerful
economic growth that had made the country a Mecca for the
world's underprivileged millions. And more than that, it has
been the feeling of pushing back frontiers, be they land frontiers in the West or space frontiers in the skies, that has ignited
the spirit of the nation and set it apart from other nations. The
drive toward expansion and growth has defined the United
States during its 200–year history, and the new efforts to cut
back, lower expectations, and retreat into the self go against the
grain of the people.

What is now needed for the United States is a rekindling of
that spirit and that national drive. A rallying point is needed to
draw together the forces of growth, and whether the goal that
is set is the conquering of space, the oceans, or the cities themselves, it must be seen as an American goal. The challenge of
the Soviets in space over two decades ago sparked the United
States to incredible efforts in technological advance and new
production. Today, a new sense of purpose is required for the
nation. And, of course, the direction must come from a new
quality of leadership in Washington, which has been sorely lack-
ing in recent years. The United States can no longer afford
leaders who offer them either Watergate scandals or ignorance
of domestic and foreign affairs. It needs capable leaders with
vision.

For the United States to curb its current slide, it must make
some hard policy choices to confront at least three main challenges in the 1980s:

• Rising foreign competition. The era when U.S. multinationals
held sway over the international markets is over, and heavy
pressure from European, Japanese, and Third World corporations for markets, oil, and raw materials is severely cutting into
the operations of American companies overseas. Just as impor-

tant, foreign technology has improved to the point where it is equal to, and even sometimes ahead of, American industrial and scientific know-how. There is now a continuing fight to reach the technological heights in the next decade, and U.S. multinationals are falling behind.

• Weakening dollar. It is clear that a plummeting dollar means much higher inflation for the country; higher oil prices as OPEC tries to recoup losses on the decline of its paper assets denominated in dollars; greater protectionism as foreign countries scramble to huddle behind capital and currency walls; and the probable destruction of the global financial system in the near future if the trend is not reversed. Right now, the dollar is an anemic world reserve currency, and its decline and instability can only bring about less international trade and more international economic anarchy.

• Energy. The skyrocketing cost of oil caused by OPEC's cartel has sent investment falling, inflation soaring, the dollar sliding, and the world as a whole reeling since 1974. At first, OPEC merely quadrupled the price of energy to the major industrial nations of the world. Now it is limiting supply, thereby threatening all future growth. The economic and military well-being of the United States is precariously dependent on the volatile politics of a handful of Mideast countries ruled, in many cases, by royal families and dictators who are doomed, as modernization continues in that region, to be overthrown and replaced by other groups. As the overthrow of the Shah of Iran showed us, conflicts following revolutions can produce forces that will cut back the supply of oil in the future and threaten not only America but Europe, Japan, and the developing countries as well.

Before the United States can reassert itself on the international scene it must drastically change the way it operates domestically. Economic policy in America for the past decade has been based on the assumption that government can give all things to all people at the same time. The inflationary consequences of the attempt to fight both a foreign war in Vietnam and launch a domestic Great Society program proved that, despite the tremendous strength of the nation, choices have to be made. In recent years, Washington policy has been centered on redistributing existing wealth through government taxation; the entire thrust of legislation has been to divide the products of an existing economy into more even shares. The quality of economic growth has been ignored in Washington, and what real expansion has occurred has been fueled by inflation-fired consumer spending bolstered by an incredible burst of debt financing. This type of consumer-led growth has led to higher imports and balance-of-payments deficits, small capital investment in domestic industry, a lower dollar, and a decline in competitiveness of U.S. goods overseas.

For the United States to reverse its decline in power it must first regain the economic strength on which its power rests. The most serious flaw in Washington today is its failure to see the links between inflation, an energy shortage, payments deficits, a declining dollar, and continued high unemployment. More than that, it doesn't see the root cause behind all the various problems—the erosion of productivity in the economy. While Washington has been acting the fireman both within the U.S. and abroad, trying to dampen the crises of the dollar, oil, inflation, and trade, it has failed to see that behind the smoke is a huge fire, set off by the fall in U.S. productivity and its competitiveness around the world.

Productivity has dropped so far that, unless it is reversed in the 1980s, the average American's standard of living is going to drop drastically. The Joint Economic Committee (JEC) of Congress recently warned that greater output per man-hour is the "economic linchpin of the 1980s." The JEC projected that if major changes did not take place soon, by 1989 a gallon of gas could cost $5.80, a house might cost $151,200, and a loaf of bread $2.06. It said that slow growth and low productivity would hit blacks, Hispanics, and other minorities especially hard.

In the first half of 1979, productivity fell by an annual rate of 3.3 percent for the whole private business sector and a whopping 5.7 percent for nonfarm business, which was the largest decline ever recorded since 1947. And though the nation's productivity did rise by 5.3 percent in 1977, it edged up by only 4.4 percent in 1978. Even more important, U.S. productivity is lagging way behind that of Japan, Europe, and even many NICs. Japan and Europe are even more dependent on OPEC oil imports for energy than is the United States, but they can pay for that oil easily with massive exports of goods that are more competitive than American products. Their currencies are strong because of balance-of-payments surpluses, and their inflation rates are lower, as well.

The key economic policy change needed, of course, is a switching away from the Depression-born Keynesian policies that emphasized pumping up inadequate demand of consumers to concentrating on producing the supply of goods and services actually used. The history of the American economy in recent years has been one of steadily declining expenditures for research and development to create new, better, and less expensive products, and of low investment in factories and modern equipment. If anything, old industries like steel have, in effect, been liquidating themselves, rather than attempting to meet the competition from abroad by modernizing and changing.

Changing this trend toward lagging productivity will be much harder than most businessmen and government officials now believe. The two policies that are most often discussed as a cure for low productivity are higher government tax credits for building new plants and equipment plus faster depreciation of older facilities. Unfortunately, these quick fixes will not do the trick, because the decline in productivity has deep social and political roots that hark back to the days of the Depression and the street riots of the 1960s.

Shocked by the millions of unemployed in the 1930s, and scared by the street riots of the 1960s, the government put forth economic policies that have been directed at redistributing income and ensuring a more egalitarian society. In recent years, the government has also undertaken to ensure that America's environment is cleaned up, not polluted. Both goals are important, but they have been implemented in a fashion that has cut down productivity, institutionalized inflation, and eroded the competitiveness of U.S. goods in the international markets. The tax policies and regulations of the government have proved to be antigrowth in nature, and different groups within the country have been fighting for their pieces of a smaller economic pie.

To raise productivity, the country has got to shift its attention away from the governmental toward the private sectors of society. Resources now going for consumption must be moved toward investment. Specifically, there must be a new flow of investment in factories and equipment to lower manufacturing costs. This would fight inflation, provide more jobs, and strengthen the competitiveness of U.S. goods abroad. Corporations are now more concerned about the fast buck than about future investment. They are more interested in buying other companies or their own stock than in planning for the next century. The personal desire to build long-standing commercial or industrial empires has faded before the need to produce quick profits for the quarterly earnings reports. Creating something is less important than managing. Bigness is almost a goal in itself, despite the fact that bureaucracy is anathema to creativity, growth, and flexibility. Risk-taking has declined, and the adventure of creating and running a business has lost its appeal.

One way to get private business moving again is to increase spending on research and development. Many of the fastest-growing companies in the United States are spin-offs from recent technological innovations. Silicon Valley in California, where dozens of small companies are turning out semiconductors and microprocessors, is one of the most exciting and competitive areas of the American economy. As old industries like steel and textiles decline and cut jobs, these new computer-based industries are hiring thousands. There should be many more such industries around the country. Technology should be applied to developing new energy sources and new sources of raw materials. The United States has been losing its lead in research and development (R & D) for years. The Japanese are closing in on computer technology; the Europeans are concentrating on aerospace; and, of course, the United States has just given up on nuclear technology and will soon be eclipsed by the Germans and the French.

In fact, U.S. spending for research and development has actually declined from 3 percent of the GNP in the mid 1960s to only 2 percent in the 1970s. While our expenditures were shrinking, spending on R & D overseas grew to the point where German, Japanese, and Soviet spending equals or surpasses that 2 percent figure. In addition, a larger amount of American R & D spending on the part of private industry is going into "defensive" research to protect corporations from violating the government's environmental restrictions. Monsanto, for example, says that up to 40 percent of its research on agricultural chemicals is devoted to meeting governmental regulations. Overseas, spending on R & D has been focused on commercially marketable products.

Beyond just the numbers of dollars spent on R & D, the United States has been falling behind in the area of new patents. American patents awarded to foreign inventors in the past ten years have doubled, and foreign patents awarded to U.S. inventors has fallen by 25 percent.

A major way to raise productivity in America would be to reverse the trend of declining spending on R & D. Private industry's spending for research and development has gone up an average of about 4 percent since 1966, but government funding has fallen 5.5 percent annually. Overall levels have fallen behind the rate of inflation.

Government spending in R & D especially should be increased immediately. Government research has led to integrated circuit technology, wide-bodied jet planes, advanced telecommunications equipment, computers, and an entire range of the most technologically advanced products in the marketplace. Higher spending for research and development is crucial to greater productivity.

Once the United States begins to move to increase its domestic productivity, it can turn to face the outside world and fight for a larger share of the world product. It is absolutely essential for the United States in the decade ahead to overhaul completely its current position on trade. The indifference toward trade by Washington policy-makers has to come to an end, and the crucial role of exports in the health of America has to be impressed on Congress. Right now, export markets are too easily sacrificed to accommodate other policies that have greater voter appeal. But U.S. payments overseas for oil imports alone ran to $65 billion in 1979 and will surely hit $100 billion by 1981. That one-year oil import bill dwarfs the entire $88 billion synthetic-fuel proposal put forth by the Carter administration. The oil import bill comes to 5 percent of the whole U.S. gross national product and 20 percent of the federal budget. In real terms, it amounts to an incredibly large movement of potential growth away from the United States and toward OPEC. Unless the United States unfurls the sails of the Yankee clipper and begins a truly massive drive to expand exports in the global markets, there is no possible way of continuing to pay for the oil import bill without seriously draining the country of real wealth, severely cutting its economic growth, and putting tremendous political pressure on the democratic process.

The shift in policy on trade and exports has to come first from Washington. So far, no administration—Democratic or Republican—has given more than tentative and extremely weak support to programs that supplement private market financing of exports. This is in the face of overwhelming evidence that foreign governments offer substantial direct and indirect assistance to their own corporations. Despite the Carter administration's verbal commitment to exports, no real action has been taken. Although the administration recommended a modest increase in the Export-Import Bank's authorized loans, it did nothing to cut down on the environmental regulations that influence its support for overseas projects. The United States nearly lost a major nuclear-power deal in the Philippines because of its desire to impose American environmental concerns on other countries. No action has been taken by the Justice Department to provide guidelines to American businessmen in dealing with the Foreign Corrupt Practices Act, outlawing bribery overseas. Of course, Europeans and the Japanese have no such laws on their books, and U.S. corporations can't even get the government to help them interpret the strict antibribery legislation, which is costing the country billions in foreign sales each year.

The Carter administration did submit a proposal to reorganize the bureaucracies that now have some control over trade. At least that was an improvement over previous neglect of the issue. But instead of centralizing authority to streamline trade policy, the proposal divides responsibility for trade between the Commerce Department and the special trade representative. In short, Washington has not yet overcome its intrabureaucratic squabbles in order to devise a simple policy-making group to plan a renewed export drive. Until that is done, no one will have overall responsibility for trade, and decision-making will remain spread all over Washington. Senator Abraham Ribicoff's (D.-Conn.) bill concentrating the scattered responsibilities for trade into a new Department of Trade would be an excellent first step.

In addition, the U.S. attitude toward the renewed rise of

protectionism has to change. Although the recent Tokyo round of trade negotiations succeeded in cutting tariffs and establishing new codes of conduct for dealing with some old trade problems, little progress was made in coming to grips with the rise of neomercantilist barriers. Unlike seventeenth- and eighteenth-century mercantilism, nations are not relying on quotas or tariffs to protect jobs and profits. They are using much more subtle mechanisms, such as indirect financial aid, low-cost credits, cartel-like schemes, currency manipulation, and "voluntary" export restraints to protect local industries. But there is very little movement in breaking down these new barriers. If anything, the United States has helped build them up by forcing Japan, Europe, and many of the NICs voluntarily to restrict their exports to the United States of steel, TVs, and many other products. And as for the multilateral trade negotiations completed in 1979, "these agreements do close some loopholes and make more explicit arbitrary trade practices," conceded Jean J. Boddewyn, professor of international commerce at Baruch College in New York. "But they also simply codify protectionism."

In Washington, there isn't even the glimmer of recognition that a problem with neomercantilism exists. With exports, at least, policy-makers are making noises about a shift in government actions. But with rising protectionism, there is a political stake in pretending it isn't a problem. Many economists in the Carter administration believe protectionism is actually on the decline. "Some individual barriers are going up, but with the new trade negotiations, there have been reductions on net," said Assistant Treasury Secretary for International Affairs Bergsten. But even Bergsten conceded that the competition overseas is becoming so stiff that some disturbing economic distortions are emerging. "There is a growing trend to manipulate the flow of investment by offering various incentives and then imposing performance requirements," he noted.

With the world splitting up into regional trading blocs revolving around the German mark, Japanese yen, and the weakening dollar, the United States must do everything possible to keep open the channels of trade and capital. It must demand reciprocity on investments and foreign sales. It must push foreign, government-owned airlines to purchase U.S. planes as well as those produced locally if U.S. planes are less expensive and better. It must push government-owned utilities, such as the Nippon Telephone and Telegraph Company, to open up its purchasing practices to U.S. corporations, which are now virtually excluded. It must insist that the OECD credit rule, which calls for nations to put a floor on the interest rates charged on their export credits, be adhered to and that current Japanese and European cheap-credit practices be stopped.

One step the United States could take to improve its trade position would be to follow the advice of the Senate Subcommittee on International Finance, which recommends:

• an investment tax credit for research and development, since 40 percent of all U.S. exports are "high-tech" products;

• extension of the domestic international sales corporations (DISCs), which help U.S. multinationals export overseas;

• the parallel use of Export-Import Bank funds with DISC money to multiply the export punch of the DISC incentives;

• deferment of taxes on sales overseas that are attributed to an export sales subsidy;

• continued exemption from taxation of some types of personal income and expenses for U.S. citizens working abroad.

Just as the U.S. can no longer ignore the impact of international trade on the domestic economy, so it can no longer ignore the global ramifications of the dollar crisis. The movement out of the dollar that began in 1978 has now turned into a stampede. Foreigners question whether America has the political leadership to fight inflation, especially in an election year, if it means sacrificing jobs. Investors overseas doubt whether the United States still has the will and the ability to lead the West after Vietnam, Watergate, and the decline of the American economy. Diversification out of the dollar is the keynote among all

global investors, ranging from the OPEC central banks to rich
individuals operating through the bankers of Switzerland.
There is no way the United States can now reverse this trend
in the early 1980s. Its immediate goal must be to establish a
process of orderly retreat away from the dollar and hope that
the domestic actions it takes in the decade ahead can set the
stage for a return of the dollar to stage-center by the end of the
1980s. That return is crucial not only for the United States,
which suffers higher inflation as the dollar weakens, but for the
world as a whole. With the decline of the dollar, the international financial system is slowly shifting toward a multireserve-
currency system, and this can be extremely dangerous. The last
time the industrial world found itself in a floating-rate system
without a single major currency as the central reserve currency
for the world, chaos ensued. That time was in the interwar
period, when sterling—dominant for two centuries—declined,
just as the dollar is declining today. And the result was competitive devaluations and trade wars.

But for now, there is little to be done except to make plans
for an orderly retreat. So sharp has been the decline of U.S.
economic power that the country can no longer sustain the
dollar overseas as the sole reserve currency. Right now, 80
percent of all foreign exchange holdings by central banks and
80 percent of the Eurocurrency markets are in dollars. Yet the
American share of world GNP has been cut in half since the
early 1960s, to only 35 percent of the total GNP of the industrial
nations. Moreover, the U.S. share of world trade has dropped to
16 percent, down from 21 percent just a few years ago and down
even more than in the 1960s. The decline in American economic might can no longer sustain the dollar, and, in fact, the
dollar's exposed position in the international financial system
has made the United States even more vulnerable than before
to foreign shocks.

The U.S. dollar strategy for the 1980s should concentrate first
on the building of a global multireserve-currency system in

which the dollar plays a major but not a central role. At the present time, there are only two other currencies that can take up some of the slack as the dollar weakens: the German mark and the Japanese yen. And, indeed, diversification out of the dollar has meant that cash has been flowing largely into these two currencies. The German and Japanese economies have shown that they can keep inflation within moderate bounds, sustain a modest rate of growth, and still pay for enormous oil imports—three goals the United States has had a very difficult time attaining.

Unfortunately, both Germany and Japan have shown little inclination to permit their money to become reserve currencies. The central banks of both nations have bitterly fought a rearguard action against the trend, despite tremendous market pressures to make the mark and yen more important in world finance.

One of the necessary steps toward making a currency a global reserve unit is to have sophisticated money markets that allow investors to put their cash into that currency and receive some interest on the investment. The United States, of course, has the world's most developed money markets, and foreigners can put their cash into U.S. Government Treasury bills (T-bills), bank certificates of deposit (CDs), and other very liquid dollar-denominated investment instruments. They can be sure that, because of the depth of the U.S. markets, they can almost always get their cash out.

But for years the Japanese and Germans have fought against the creation of sophisticated money markets specifically to prevent the yen and mark from joining the dollar as reserve currencies. Neither wanted the problems associated with strong reserve currencies: overvaluation and loss of control of domestic money supply. And both sought to stop their banks from issuing any liquid money-market instruments, like CDs, and creating a real money market. In 1978, the German central bank stepped in at the very last moment and forbade Germany's DG Bank from selling mark-denominated CDs in New York, and in the fall of 1979 it put the squeeze on German banks in Luxembourg that were selling short-term mark notes to foreign central banks. In both cases, the demand for mark-denominated short-term assets came from institutions trying to diversify their portfolios instead of relying solely on the dollar.

U.S. policy must concentrate on pushing both Germany and Japan to take on more of the responsibility of the world economy by allowing the existing market forces to work and make the mark and yen reserve currencies. This won't be easy, but already the Japanese are loosening up a bit to permit the creation of a yen CD market in Tokyo. While the Germans procrastinate, the Japanese are permitting big dollar-holders to go into yen assets.

But in the end, the United States must strive to make the retreat of the dollar only a temporary phenomenon, and aim for a new international monetary system in which, by the end of the decade, the dollar will once again play a central role. The years ahead will be extremely dangerous as long as the dollar remains weak and the global financial system rests on a multireserve-currency system. As economist Robert Mundell of Columbia University put it: "What is developing is a currency oligopoly dominated by the United States, Germany, and Japan, and this could be very unhealthy." And Anthony Solomon, undersecretary of the Treasury for monetary affairs under Carter, agreed: "A multireserve system would be very volatile and even more unstable than what exists now." But the United States has no choice for the moment. It has declined to the point where it can no longer hope to preserve the dollar's special status. It must work for a short-term retreat while making serious efforts to reinvigorate the economy for a comeback in the late 1980s.

Above all, U.S. energy policy in the 1980s must aim at reducing the country's dependence on Mideast oil, and on Saudi Arabian oil in particular. Unfortunately, the options for the years immediately ahead are severely limited. There is not going to be any single or simple way to achieve energy independence for America in the coming decade. U.S. energy policy must rely instead on a combination of efforts to cut down on its external dependence.

First, the decline of U.S. oil and gas production must be stemmed and, if possible, reversed. The direct use of coal must be encouraged, and, where economical, the government should encourage the production of synthetic fuels from shale and coal. Just as important, conservation can be a powerful force in itself, and the country should make every effort to harness and direct it. Finally, the United States should act, as a matter of foreign policy, to foster oil exploration and production in foreign countries outside the Middle East and perhaps outside OPEC. The major effort now being undertaken off the shore of China by U.S. oil exploration companies should be expanded to every part of the globe where the potential for new sources of oil exists.

The transition from an economy built on cheap energy to one in which energy is expensive will be painful, but it is the first and necessary step up from the decline of U.S. power. The government has already made an important change by starting the decontrol of crude-oil and natural-gas prices. Decontrol itself will have a salutary effect by encouraging conservation through higher prices for energy. But the United States will have to go further and decontrol gasoline prices as well, accepting $2.00 a gallon gas. The second important step the government now must make is to return a large proportion of the proposed windfall profits tax to the oil companies. The extra cash generated by decontrol must, to a large degree, be made available to the corporations in charge of providing energy. Despite the fact that recent drilling efforts have not led to greater oil production, the money can be used for synthetic-fuel development and further exploration in both the United States and abroad.

However, it will take more than just higher profits for the oil companies to get synthetic-fuel plants built; it will call for government help. The risk that oil prices may decline, the environmental problems, and the capital costs, all require government involvement in synfuels. Synthetic-fuel plants will have a two-fold purpose. They will, of course, cut down on U.S. imports of foreign oil. But perhaps just as important, they will mark symbolically the American effort to achieve energy independence in the 1980s. The real cost of U.S. dependence on foreign oil goes way beyond the $65 billion to $100 billion the country pays. The cost must be seen in terms of the declining dollar, continued instability in the Middle East, and domestic inflation. The high cost of synthetic fuels must be judged in these real terms.

Finally, nuclear energy must be given a second chance. Serious mistakes have been made by both the private and public sectors in calculating the cost of, and in providing for safeguards in the use of, atomic power. But it remains one important means of reducing America's dependence on foreign energy. The Three Mile Island nuclear plant accident could be a new beginning for atomic power if it is used to stimulate anew the technology of the industry, which still relies on designs drawn up in the 1950s. If the plants can be made truly safe and cost-competitive with other sources of energy, then America should continue to use atomic power as one way of reducing its dependence on foreign oil imports.

Beyond a massive shift in U.S. policies on trade, the dollar, and energy, one of the most important social changes that may have to take place if the United States is to reverse its decline of power is the creation of a new set of relationships among government, the multinational corporation, and labor. In order for America to compete overseas, a closer association between the public and private sectors is essential. A redefinition of the ties between the political and the economic systems of the country is needed if the United States is to compete in the international arena and survive. Without question, any such move is fraught with danger insofar as it threatens to change the traditional political alignment of power in the country. But there is already some movement in the direction of closer ties. Recently, Senator Lowell Weicker (R.-Conn.) said, "I'm tired of hearing of Japan Inc. I want to usher in American Inc. I don't want monopolies at home. I want competition. But if it takes monopolization to improve our balance of trade and flex our economic muscle abroad, I want to see our industries able to act in concert abroad—with the federal government as their foreign business partner."

The need for a much closer relationship among business, labor, and government stems less from domestic pressures than from forces acting overseas. When the United States was supreme in the 1950s and 1960s, its corporations were able to compete in a relatively free environment. After World War II, the United States had proceeded to set the rules of the global game and enforce them. American multinationals played according to those rules—and met no competition from foreign corporations for two decades.

This all began to change in the late 1960s. Just as Japanese and European multinationals were beginning to move abroad to vie with their American counterparts for a share of the international national product, the U.S. Government was beginning to shift to an adversary relationship with U.S. corporations. The effort of the government to put on capital controls in the mid-1960s because of pressure on the dollar threatened to dry up the financing needed by U.S. multinationals in their expansion. The attempt by the government to impose post-Watergate morality on corporate activities abroad has led to antibribery legislation that not only has hindered corporate sales overseas but has discredited dozens of executives who thought they were only playing by the rules. And, finally, the antipollution regulations and bureaucratic red tape of recent years has firmly put the government at odds with corporations who complain about

these curbs on growth. All this has added up to a business attitude toward government that is very simple: "Just keep Washington off our back."

But that desire by business to keep government at arm's
length is now changing under pressure from overseas. And that
change may form the basis for a new social contract between
government and business that will reshape the future of the
nation.

U.S. multinationals increasingly find that their foreign corporate competitors in the global markets often have the invisible
hand of government behind them in secret aid. European and
Japanese governments have very close ties with their corporations, many of which are partly or wholly owned by the state,
and foreign policy is made up, to a large degree, of efforts to
promote national exports or investments. On one level, foreign
governments provide low-cost credit and manipulate currencies to create the conditions for healthy trade for their corporations. On another level, governments use economic policy as a
basic tool of foreign policy and try to push the interests of
national corporations and industries around the world. British,
French, German, and Japanese embassies regularly promote
products and big economic deals in the Middle East and Third
World. Wherever he travels abroad, President Valéry Giscard
d'Estaing normally carries a large economic package that may
help French industry, exports, and employment. In short,
American corporations are finding that they face on their own
the combined power not only of private foreign corporate competitors but of foreign governments, too. And competing in that
environment has proved to be extremely difficult.

Cries for more U.S. Government help in competing abroad
have become common among American businessmen, and a
basis for a new type of relationship between business and government, with labor an integral part, now exists. In this new
relationship, multinational corporations might expect several

things from Washington. First, Washington could make an active effort to promote U.S. products and investments overseas. Embassies could become involved in offering to local countries large package deals drawn up with corporations. Just as the Common Market is now negotiating as a unit with OPEC for a deal involving long-term contracts for oil exports in exchange for technology transfers, guaranteed markets for OPEC products, and even military equipment, so the U.S. can offer such programs to an individual nation and on a regional basis. For this to work, administration officials up to the President would have to follow the example of the French and sell American products around the world.

The government could also offer a much greater amount of low-cost trade financing through the Export-Import Bank. Many American multinationals complain that they lose out constantly to foreign MNCs, which can offer much cheaper financing for both projects and specific products. For example, China was able to get $17 billion in government-guaranteed credits in 1979 to finance imports of technology and plants. In addition, it got $3.5 billion in commercial bank credits. France extended $7 billion in credit to buy French goods; Britain, $5 billion; Japan, $2 billion, with promises of double that amount to come; Italy, $1 billion; Canada, $2.3 billion; and even Sweden came in with $350 million. Nearly a year after the Europeans and Japanese offered these credits to China, the United States promised only $2 billion sometime in the future.

Something else the government can offer business in a new relationship is a change of attitude toward big business. It will take a great deal of educating in Washington, but somehow the picture of the type of competition going on in the international market among giant multinational corporations must be made clear. The U.S. Government is the only government in the world that is still trying to break up its corporate giants, and the current attempt to break up IBM only comforts Japanese computer-makers in Tokyo. Around the world, governments are

trying to centralize industries they see as vital to future industrialization and trade—not break them apart. As Arjay Miller,
the retired dean of the Stanford Business School put it: "The
Japanese had 13 firms in the auto-manufacturing business in
1963. With government encouragement, the number has been
reduced to three or four and you can see the results all about
you on the roads."

Of course, an American move toward lowering the adversary
relationship between the government and business has its risks.
Europe is full of government-owned industries that lose billions
of dollars annually, from British Steel to Italy's Montedison.
They are kept running to provide employment, with few prospects of ever turning a profit. They will never be competitive
or innovative. Whatever new relationship corporations and
Washington create between themselves, there must remain
free play of markets to provide the flexibility that is crucial in
international competition. If the government acts merely to
protect dying industries, then the new partnership will be a
failure and American competitiveness will fall even further.

As part of its change in attitude toward business, government
will also have to give up its efforts to force a new morality on
corporate activities around the world. Bribery in the United
States is obviously illegal, but gift-giving is not only the way
things are done in many cultures around the world; it is the only
method of getting anything done. U.S. corporations abroad
should be selling American products and services. How they go
about it, short of toppling governments, should be defined in
terms of how business is done in a particular foreign country.
The Germans, Japanese, British, and French do not have legislation that penalizes their corporations for offering cash for contracts overseas. Only the United States insists on hamstringing
its multinationals in a naïve effort to export American post-
Watergate morality. One congressional study estimated that
the antibribery legislation alone has cost the United States $1
billion annually in overseas sales over the past two years, and

the real sum may be substantially higher. America, in the post-imperial era, simply cannot afford the luxury of being holier-than-thou.

Corporations, for their part, can offer several things to the government within the context of a new relationship. In exchange for Washington's aid, corporations may have to change their global operations to emphasize exporting from the continental United States instead of producing abroad. American multinationals have a huge investment, totaling nearly $200 billion, in plants and equipment overseas, and exporting from the United States may mean competing at times with their own subsidiaries. But if the United States is to work its way up from its current weakness, exports must play a very large role in economic policy. Yet the biggest multinational corporations may, in fact, be threatened by a large export-promotion campaign because so many of their activities are abroad. In the end, corporations may have to change their own internal sales and marketing and production strategies to redirect resources away from a global distribution toward an American base. They may have to give up some of their stake in manufacturing and exporting from foreign bases in order to produce in, and export from, the United States.

But exporting from the United States may prove to be very hard for many American corporations. Critics of the management policies of U.S. multinationals argue that they are often unable to compete in the complex and competitive world trade markets. Often, they are so used to building things and selling them within the confines of the huge continental U.S. market that they lack the initiative and imagination to compete against the Japanese and Europeans. What they do abroad is frequently for the home market. "American car-makers manufacture just for the American market," said Honda Motor Car's Michihiro Nishida, executive vice-president. "They don't have any market in mind other than the United States. But the real multinational enterprise must keep in mind such things as Japanese having the steering wheel on the right side," Nishida added, with a sigh. U.S. car exports to Japan hardly ever take into account that the Japanese picked up their driving habits from the British, not the Americans, and drive on the left, not right.

Beyond that, corporations may have to provide a specific social service in exchange for government support, and that could be in the sensitive area of minority employment. The United States—despite its 200-year history—is still a country struggling to become a nation. Germany, Japan, Switzerland, South Korea, and other nations are able to draw on all the resources of their united, homogeneous populations in the drive to produce and trade. The United States, meanwhile, remains divided, wasting enormous social resources. Ever-higher taxes for social services have led not only to an enormously bloated government bureaucracy, but also to higher inflation. By failing truly to integrate its various groups, the United States has paid a large economic price—a price other nations do not have to pay.

Minorities still do not feel that they have a real stake in America. Despite all the government programs, the promises of the Great Society, they remain outsiders, without the motivation to use the traditional mechanism of upward mobility in the United States—education. And without motivation, no amount of formal schooling, no amount of "enrichment," is going to get them to learn the skills needed to advance in this technologically sophisticated country. Yet it may be that the United States can no longer forfeit the potential social resources of the minorities —and certainly can no longer afford its social costs—in the fight for economic and political power in the 1980s.

Private industry can help in bringing in the outside groups and furthering the integration of American society by providing the vital stake people need in society. Knowing they can "make it" in corporate America could provide minority-group members with the missing motivation for learning. The first step, of course, is employment, but that is not sufficient. What is needed for the decade ahead is a much closer relationship between education and private industry, whereby industry makes clear it is committed to offering jobs and the chance of upward advancement once people learn the proper skills.

It may be that certain corporations will have to "adopt" entire school districts and offer a specific number and variety of jobs to students who show that they have the required skills. It may be that corporations have to move into the education business themselves to provide the skills. The inner-city school systems have proved a complete failure in educating minorities, not because the schools themselves are inadequate but because the students don't have the motivation for learning. With corporations involved in education and offering the prospect of good employment and the chance to move ahead, the missing student motivation might be instilled. An informal relationship between a corporation and a school—not unlike that already existing between certain Ivy League universities and particular Wall Street legal and financial firms—could be put into effect.

Of course, there always is the danger that such an arrangement between private industry and education could result in a more inflexible labor market. The Japanese and Europeans find it very difficult ever to fire anyone, regardless of business conditions, and valuable capital that should be going into new technology often is poured back into older industries to maintain employment. On the other hand, a committed work force can increase productivity tremendously, cut inflation, and raise the economic growth rate.

By integrating the outside groups into society through private industry, the United States could save hundreds of billions of dollars in public funds now spent on social services. That cash could be channeled back into industry through lower taxes and higher spending on research and development, leading to a reinvigorated economy in the 1980s.

Of course, any new social contract between the government and private industry must include a commitment from the big labor unions for higher productivity and greater U.S. exports. To date, the big unions have concentrated solely on the safety of their members' jobs and protecting them from foreign competition. The unions have proved to be among the most vocal proponents of protectionism in the country and have shown little concern for America's competitive position abroad. An export-oriented America must fight against all protectionism, including its own, and labor must be willing to give up jobs in dying industries to gain the opportunity of receiving even more employment slots in new growth industries. It is clear that the United States does not have the competitive edge any longer in producing shoes, most textiles, steel, and many other labor-intensive products. Yet the unions have fought bitterly in Washington with great success to put up artificial barriers to preserve these antiquated industries in the United States for the sake of jobs.

In much the same way, unions have shown a lack of regard for the plummeting productivity of the country—a decline that is hurting the United States in the overseas trade markets. Right now unions do not really perceive themselves as having a big stake in fostering greater productivity in the American economy. With government policies firing up red-hot inflation, it is only natural that the unions are focusing on not falling behind in real income. But to turn the country around, that concentration on battling inflation through ever-higher cost-of-living allowances, pay raises, and fringe benefits must be shifted toward achieving greater productivity in plants across the United States. It may be that the government must first show it is willing to change its fiscal and monetary policies to fight inflation, instead of promoting it, before the unions shift their own position, but that position must be altered if the United States is to reverse its decline of power.

There is no turning back the clock on America's former dominance of the world economic order, but there are ways to stop the present slide into historical oblivion. The United States must redefine its global interests, state specifically to the world what they are, and go about protecting them. The United States must rebuild its economy to compete in an international arena where fiercely challenging nations fight for larger shares of the world product. Few nations ever get a second chance to reverse their decline in power. For the United States, the 1980s will certainly be that chance.

Note About the Authors

Index

Note About the Authors

The Decline of U.S. Power (and what we can do about it) was written by a special *Business Week* team directed by Bruce Nussbaum, associate editor of *Business Week* for International Money Management. Nussbaum is an award-winning (Deadline Club) journalist who supervises the coverage of crucial changes in the global financial markets, from the gyrating dollar to the explosive growth in demand for gold. Born in New York City, Nussbaum graduated from Brooklyn College at the City University of New York in 1967 and did graduate work in political science at the University of Michigan. Between 1967 and 1969, he lived in Southeast Asia as a Peace Corps volunteer and worked as a journalist, writing for the *Far Eastern Economic Review* on the political and economic ramifications of the Vietnam War. He joined the *American Banker* newspaper in 1974 to write the daily money-markets column, and came to *Business Week* in 1976 to head up the new International Money Management Department.

Nussbaum wrote the introduction and conclusion to *The Decline of U.S. Power,* played a major role in editing the chapter on energy, and coordinated the rest of the team of authors. He directed this first attempt to use the techniques of financial-magazine journalism to chronicle the fall of America from its postwar heights of power.

The global arena has become so specialized and interdependent, with oil and the dollar as much a part of American power as missiles or aircraft carriers, that only a carefully chosen team of journalists can now provide genuine coverage of the big picture. This team approach is used at *Business Week.* Nussbaum was at the center of the team—probably the best group of American financial journalists ever assembled—that wrote the book.

Edward M. Mervosh, *Business Week*'s European bureau chief, based in Brussels, handled the chapter entitled "The Dollar: Crumbling Cornerstone of the Alliance," and contributed greatly to the entire book. Mervosh specializes in covering the European financial scene, from the volatile Eurocurrency markets to the economic outlook for the Common Market. Prior to this assignment, he covered the Federal Reserve, the Treasury, the Office of Management and Budget, and the Council of Economic Advisers for McGraw-Hill's World News Service in Washington, D.C. Mervosh has studied economics and history at Columbia University and New York University and is a member of the National Association of Business Economists.

Jack Kramer is *Business Week*'s Cairo bureau chief, covering the crucial Middle East. A former staff reporter for the *Wall Street Journal* and editor at *Time* magazine, Kramer is the author of *Travels with the Celestial Dog,* a book about the 1960s. He reported on Africa and Asia from 1967 to 1979, when he joined *Business Week* to write on oil and politics; he covers Egypt, Saudi Arabia, Iran, the gulf states, and the rest of the Middle East.

Lenny Glynn, *Business Week*'s International Business editor, wrote the chapter on multinational corporations. He graduated from Columbia University in 1972, with a degree in political science. Before joining *Business Week* in 1978, he worked for *Time* magazine's World and International departments for three years. His dramatization for public television, *The White House Tapes,* won the 1974 Virgin Islands Film Festival award as the best documentary of the year.

Lewis Beman, a *Business Week* economics associate, worked on the chapter on energy policy. In 1958, he graduated from the University of Wisconsin, where he majored in history, and did graduate work in economics there from 1958 to 1960. He has been a close observer of the oil industry since covering the field for the McGraw-Hill Washington bureau in the early 1960s. Beman worked for *Business Week* from 1969 to 1972, joined *Fortune* magazine at that time as an associate editor, and returned to *Business Week* in 1978.

William Wolman, deputy editor of *Business Week,* provided guidance for the book and insight into the problem of the decline of U.S. power. At *Business Week,* he is responsible for integrating economic and political coverage, concentrating on the fast-breaking economic developments that are the prime concern of businessmen and governments around the world. A native of Canada, Wolman graduated from McGill University in Montreal and earned his Ph.D. in economics from Stanford University. He joined *Business Week* in 1960 and became economics editor in 1965. He left in 1969 to join Citibank as a vice-president in charge of its varied economic publications, and two years later joined Argus Research, where he forecast economic trends. He rejoined the magazine in December 1974. Wolman is co-author of the book *The Beat Inflation Strategy,* and has won the Deadline Club, John Hancock, and Newspaper Guild of New York Page One awards.

Lewis H. Young, editor-in-chief of *Business Week,* played a special role in writing the book. His thoughts on the need for higher productivity greatly influenced the last chapter, on policy prescriptions—what we can do about reversing the decline of U.S. power. Young also played a major role in shaping the concept for a special report in the magazine, which has been much amplified and updated to make this book.

Index

Mercantilism: new, 4, 16, 27, 196, 213; seventeenth-century, 155, 196
Merrow, Edward W., 88
Messerschmitt-Bölkow-Blohm (West Germany), 154
Mexico: fall of U.S. share of total trade in, 158; oil and gas reserves of, 94
Middle East: Harold Brown's 1979 trip to, 14, 56–57; combined gross national product in, 44; decline of U.S. influence in, 47–50; double-edged sword faced by U.S. in, 33–35; rise of Soviet influence in, 50–54; Soviet strategy in, 54–55; triangle, geographical delineation of, 35–37; U.S. response to Soviet strength in, 56–58
Miller, Arjay, 223
Miller, G. William, 186
Miller, Henry E., 87
Mills, D. Quinn, 91
Minford, Patrick, 190–91
Mitsubishi (Japan), 136–37
Mobil, 102, 128
Monroe Doctrine, 116
Monsanto, 131, 210
Monsanto Europe, 156
Montecatini (Italy), 133
Montedison (Italy), 133, 223
Moore, John L., 151
Morgan Guaranty Trust Company, 19, 164
Morrison-Knudsen Company, 38
Mossadegh, Mohammed, 103
Moynihan, Daniel Patrick, 6, 21
Mozambique, 143; sale of locomotives to, 151
Multicurrency reserve system, 164, 215–16
Multinational corporations, U.S., 7–8, 205–6; in Canada, 129–30; consequences of Vietnam War for, 124–26; criticism of, 123–24; decline of, 4, 115–16, 141–42, 152–60; European response to, 130–33; history of growth of, 116–23; hostility of U.S. policy toward, 145–52; impact of dynamism of newly industrialized

countries on, 138–41; impact of European multinationals on, 132–35; impact of Japan's resurgence as exporter and investor on, 135–38, 141; impact of worldwide revolutionary movements on, 142–45; influence of, on world economy, 115; need for closer relationship among government, labor, and, 219–28; in nuclear industries, complaints from, 152–53; scandals involving, 126–27; takeover of, by host governments, 127–29; Third World analysis of, 127; and U.S. Export-Import Bank, 150–52
Mundell, Robert, 217
Municipalities and Rural Affairs Ministry (Saudi Arabia), 39
Muslim Brotherhood, 71
Muslim resurgence. See Islamic resurgence
Mutaab, Prince, 40

Nasser, Gamal Abdel, 35, 58, 59
National Energy Board (Canada), 94–95
National Iranian Oil Company, 67
National Westminster Bank Ltd. (London), 172
Naveja, Albert F., 167–68
Nayef, Prince, 40
Nazir, Hisham, 41, 43, 45
Nestlé, 135
Netherlands, 154; aid to Egypt from, 58; foreign subsidiaries of, 132; support of, for the Sudan, 53
Newly industrialized countries (NICs): impact of dynamism of, on U.S. multinationals, 138–41; productivity gains of, 208
Nicaragua, deposing of Somoza in, 143
Nigeria, cutback in oil production in, 20
Nimeiry, Jaafer Mohammed al-, 51–53, 69
Nippon Telephone and Telegraph Company, 214
Nishida, Michihiro, 224–25

Nissan (Japan), 155

Nixon, Richard M., 85, 98, 99, 153; and decline of dollar, 172, 178–81; New Economic Policy of, 179; Project Independence of, 14, 87; resignation of, 142; and Vietnam War, 124, 125; visit of, to Soviet Union, 146; wage-price controls of, 125, 179, 181, 185, 191; and Watergate, 2, 99, 126

Nixon Doctrine, 12–13, 144

Norris Industries, Incorporated, 89

North Atlantic Treaty Organization (NATO), 49, 54, 118

North Yemen: conflicts between South Yemen and, 48, 50; U.S. arms for, 14

Nuclear power: disappointment of, 85–86; need for second chance for, 219

Oasis Oil Company, 106

Occidental Petroleum, 87, 106, 108, 204

Office of Management and Budget, 100–101

Ohira, Masayoshi, 34

Oil: American dependence on foreign, 1, 3, 18, 22; crisis, American response to, 75–77; cutbacks in production of, 20–21; falling of, into hostile hands, 34; from glut to scarcity of, 107–12; imports, U.S., 14, 211; Iranian, 42, 67; Iraqi, 44, 64–65; Libyan price hike in (1970), 107–9; North Sea and Alaskan, 20; outer continental shelf (OCS) drilling in, 82–83; prices, decontrol of U.S., 83–84, 218; prorating system for, 102; reserves, fall in world, 77–84; Saudi Arabian, 42–45; and Seven Sisters, 101–4; swapping of gold for, 25–27, 80. *See also* Organization of Petroleum Exporting Countries

Oil companies: failure of OCS drilling by, 82–83; oil crisis blamed on, 75; seven mammoth, 17, 101–4; takeover of multinational, by host governments, 128; windfall profits tax proposed for, 83, 84 and n, 97, 218

Olympics, 1980 Moscow, 147

Oman, tensions between South Yemen and, 48, 50

OPEC. *See* Organization of Petroleum Exporting Countries

Organization of African Unity (OAU), 51

Organization for Economic Cooperation and Development (OECD), 182, 183, 190, 214

Organization of Petroleum Exporting Countries (OPEC), 9, 43, 202, 203; American dependence on oil from, 1, 3; American response to oil price hikes by, 75–77; Common Market's negotiations with, 222; continued raising of cost of oil by, 3, 13, 18, 89; European and Japanese dependence on oil from, 22–23, 208; impact of, on American inflation, 3, 5, 6; impact of U.S. synfuels program on, 91; oil price hike of (1973–1974), 11, 18–19, 99–100, 171, 181; oil price hike of (1978–1979), 12, 14, 18–19, 156, 185, 188, 192; rise to power of, 104–7, 109–12; strategies for dealing with threat of, 91–96; supply of oil limited by, 20, 206

Otaiba, Mana Saeed al-, 22

Outer continental shelf (OCS), failure of drilling in, 82–83

Palestine Liberation Organization (PLO), 18, 21–22, 39

Palestinians: and Camp David Egyptian-Israeli peace treaty, 18, 36, 49, 60; in Kuwait, 39; relation between oil problems and, 18, 21

Pechiney (France), 133

Pepsico, 146

PetroCanada, 129–30

Petroleum Industry Research Foundation, 107

Petroleum Intelligence Weekly, 22